MATH
FOR ALL

Participant Book
Grades
3–5

MATH
FOR ALL

Participant Book

Grades 3–5

Babette Moeller
Barbara Dubitsky
Marvin Cohen
Karen Marschke-Tobier
Hal Melnick
Linda Metnetsky

A Joint Publication

CORWIN
A SAGE Company

Education Development Center, Inc.

Bank Street

CORWIN
A SAGE Company

FOR INFORMATION:

Corwin
A SAGE Company
2455 Teller Road
Thousand Oaks, California 91320
(800) 233-9936
Fax: (800) 417-2466
www.corwin.com

SAGE Ltd.
1 Oliver's Yard
55 City Road
London EC1Y 1SP
United Kingdom

SAGE India Pvt. Ltd.
B 1/I 1 Mohan Cooperative Industrial Area
Mathura Road, New Delhi 110 044
India

SAGE Asia-Pacific Pte. Ltd.
33 Pekin Street #02-01
Far East Square
Singapore 048763

Acquisitions Editor: Dan Alpert
Associate Editor: Megan Bedell
Editorial Assistant: Sarah Bartlett
Production Editor: Veronica Stapleton
Typesetter: C&M Digitals (P) Ltd.
Proofreader: Scott Oney
Cover Designer: Karine Hovsepian
Permissions Editor: Karen Ehrmann

Library of Congress Cataloging-in-Publication Data

Math for all participant book (3-5) / Babette Moeller... [et al.].

p. cm.
"A joint publication with Educational Development Center and Bank Street College of Education."

ISBN 978-1-4129-9521-4 (pbk.)

1. Individualized instruction. 2. Mathematics—Study and teaching (Middle school)—Activity programs. I. Moeller, Babette.

QA20.I53M38 2011
510.71'2—dc23   2011020066

This book is printed on acid-free paper.

11 12 13 14 15 10 9 8 7 6 5 4 3 2 1

Contents

Acknowledgments

We are grateful to the following individuals and organizations for their contributions to the materials in this book:

We are deeply indebted to Cindy Wang, Cristian Solorza, Natalie Dean, Rebecca Caban, Danita Wright, Maria Botto, and Vilma Caban, the teachers of the five case lessons that form the core of the Grade 3–5 workshops, for opening their classrooms and sharing their practices with us and the community of *Math for All* participants. The adapted student worksheets included in workshops 1, 2, 4, and 5 were created by them. A special thanks to Cindy Wang for the sample classroom rules included in workshop 4. We also would like to express our great appreciation to the students in the teachers' classrooms for allowing us and *Math for All* participants to learn from them. Samples of their work are included in workshops 1, 2, and 4.

We thank Hal Melnick for creating the memory game, and Linda Metnetsky for developing the master design activity.

We are very grateful to Pearson Education and McGraw Hill, publishers of the *Investigations in Number, Data, and Space* and *Everyday Mathematics* curricula, for granting us permission to reprint the curriculum guides for the case lessons that are being discussed in the *Math for All* workshops.

A special thank you to Louisa Anderson for helping to format and organize the materials in this book and for obtaining permissions for reprints. We are also deeply grateful for the countless hours she has spent, with the help of our interns Cassandra Laboy and Ada Uruchima, on duplicating, organizing, and shipping draft versions of these materials to our many pilot- and field-test sites. Thank you also to our reviewers for their helpful comments and suggestions.

Last but not least, we would like to thank Dan Alpert, our editor at Corwin Press, for his thoughtful guidance and enormous patience with getting the materials in this book ready for publication.

PUBLISHER'S ACKNOWLEDGMENTS

Corwin gratefully acknowledges the contributions of the following reviewers:

June Apaza, Deputy Director
Center for the Advancement of Mathematics and Science Education
Black Hills State University
Spearfish, SD

Mark Bower, Director of Elementary Education and Staff
  Development
Hilton CSD
Hilton, NY

Thelma Davis, Principal
Robert Lunt Elementary School
Former K–5 Mathematics and Science Coordinator
Clark County, SD / Las Vegas, NV

Judith A. Filkins, K–8 Math and Science Curriculum Coordinator
Lebanon School District
Lebanon, NH

Vicki Kapust
Center for the Advancement of Mathematics and Science Education
Black Hills State University
Spearfish, SD

Maggie B. McGatha, Assistant Professor of Mathematics Education
Department of Teaching and Learning
College of Education and Human Development
University of Louisville
Louisville, KY

Edward C. Nolan, Executive Director
Maryland Council of Teachers of Mathematics
Montgomery County Public Schools
New Market, MD

Sandra S. Overcash, Math Specialist
Princess Anne Elementary School
Virginia Beach, VA

Renee Peoples, Math Instructional Facilitator
Swain County Elementary Schools
Bryson City, NC

About the Authors

Dr. Babette Moeller is a Senior Research Scientist at the Center for Children and Technology of the Education Development Center. She brings more than 25 years of experience researching and developing technology-enhanced programs in mathematics and science to help ensure that students with disabilities and those from other traditionally underrepresented groups will be included in and benefit from educational reform efforts. As project director of numerous research and development projects, Dr. Moeller has had extensive experience in designing and implementing technology-supported programs in general and special education, providing professional development for teachers and administrators in a variety of settings, and conducting formative and summative evaluation research. She also has taught courses in technology integration, media research, and child development at Fordham University's Graduate School of Education and the New School for Social Research. She currently serves as adjunct faculty in the Mathematics Leadership Program at Bank Street College of Education. Dr. Moeller holds a Ph.D. in developmental psychology from the New School for Social Research.

Dr. Barbara Dubitsky, a faculty member of the Graduate School at Bank Street College of Education, is the Director of the Mathematics Leadership Program, a program she developed in collaboration with a team of colleagues. Dr. Dubitsky has been a member of the Graduate School at Bank Street College for more than 30 years and has worked extensively in public and private schools to help teachers build their capacity to teach mathematics.

One of her major focuses is the use of technology in education, and especially how it can be used for online education. Recently she taught two short mathematics courses online. Dr. Dubitsky has worked with technology since the Bank Street College began to use computers with children in 1980, playing a key role in the Center for Children and Technology housed at Bank Street from 1980 to the early 90's. She was Chair of Computer Programs in the Graduate School. Previously, she worked for many years as a public school teacher in Grades 4 through 6, and she went on to become a middle school math teacher and math coordinator. Dr. Dubitsky holds an Ed.D. in Mathematics, Statistics, and Computing Education from Teachers College, Columbia University.

Dr. Marvin Cohen is a Senior Faculty member (Niemeyer Chair, 2005) at Bank Street College of Education and a member of the Mathematics Leadership Program (MLP) faculty. He teaches both mathematics pedagogy and content classes and advises in the MLP. Dr. Cohen, with his colleagues, helped to develop the ten video case studies that are the foundation of this Math for All curriculum, aimed at increasing access to meaningful mathematics for all children K–5. Dr. Cohen was "Scholar in Residence" at the Ben Franklin International School in Barcelona, Spain, in the spring of 2010.

Dr. Cohen has also been Director of Instructional Technology at Bank Street and has been director of a variety of technology-based projects that focus on building a technology-using environment at Bank Street. He has coordinated collaborations with Vanderbilt University and the University of Virginia. He was a co-designer of the Mathematics Learning Forums (Annenberg, 1994), a distance education project, and was a co-founder of Bank Street's Center for Minority Achievement (a middle school reform project) and the Mathematics Leadership Program.

Dr. Karen Marschke-Tobier (1942–2008) was the Director of the Early Childhood Special Education Program and a faculty member of the Graduate School at Bank Street College of Education. In addition to her appointment at Bank Street, Dr. Marschke-Tobier worked as a child therapist in private practice and served as a psychology consultant at the Corlears School for 20 years. She received her training in child psychoanalysis at the Hampstead Child Therapy Clinic in London run by Anna Freud. Dr. Marschke-Tobier also had experience as an early childhood teacher, Head Start consultant, and school social worker. Her special interests included the influence of emotions and the role of play in development and learning as well as school and family connections. Throughout her career she remained deeply committed as an advocate for children, the environment, and public education as a means of fostering change.

Dr. Hal Melnick is a faculty member of the Mathematics Leadership Program at Bank Street College of Education in New York City. He teaches courses in Math Education for new and tenured teachers and for math coaches. Dr. Melnick began his career as an elementary school teacher in the New York City public schools, where he studied in and taught Madison Project courses for NYC teachers across the city. Today he enjoys working as a mathematics professional developer in public and private schools both in the United States and internationally. His focus is on developing professional learning communities in schools, enlarging teachers' pedagogical content knowledge as they teach mathematics, and helping teachers reflect on their own beliefs about mathematics teaching and its effect on student learning. Currently he is engaged in consulting for the New York City Department of Education's Early Childhood Assessment in Math Professional Development effort. Dr. Melnick holds a Ph.D. in Mathematics Education from the Union Institute and a master's degree from Bank Street College.

 **Linda Metnetsky** is a faculty member of the Bank Street Graduate School of Education and an adviser with the Mathematics Leadership Program. At present Linda teaches Math for Teachers, Diagnosis in Mathematics, and Integrated Mathematics II. She worked extensively in the New York City public schools as a math coach and in other professional development capacities at the local and district level. She continues to work with a small public school supporting teachers in their professional development in mathematics. In addition to her involvement in the "Math for All" NSF Research Grant, she works with New York City math coaches to train teachers in ECAM, an early childhood assessment tool, and is working to create a portfolio system, a tool for formative assessment, for elementary schools.

Introduction

Welcome to the *Math for All* professional development program! This book contains all the handouts, worksheets, and curriculum materials that you, as a participant, will need to complete the five workshops that are part of this program. *Math for All* may be different from other professional development you have participated in previously, so below we describe the main goals and activities of the program to give you a better sense of what to expect.

GOALS AND PURPOSES

The *Math for All* workshop series will introduce you to a process for collaborative lesson planning that will support you in your efforts to make math lessons accessible to all students, including those with disabilities. Key components of this lesson planning process include

- analyzing the mathematical goals of the lesson you are planning for and understanding how these goals relate to the mathematics that your students studied prior to this lesson and that they will study in the future;
- analyzing the demands of the lesson;
- thinking about the strengths and needs of individual students in your classroom and how they will respond to the demands of the lesson; and
- selecting instructional strategies that address the strengths and needs of individual students in your class to make the lesson more accessible without changing the mathematical goals.

As part of the professional development, you will learn about neurodevelopmental theory (see sidebar for more detail) and how to use it as a lens to better understand the demands of math activities and individual students' strengths and needs.

Throughout the five workshops, you will be working collaboratively with one or more colleagues. Ideally, you will be working in a team that consists of at least one classroom teacher and one special education teacher who serve the same

> **The Neurodevelopmental Framework**
>
> Neurodevelopmental theory is based on the assumption that learning is not a one-dimensional process, but rather involves eight different neurodevelopmental systems or functions, which interact to enable students to acquire certain knowledge and skills, or to
>
> *(Continued)*

(Continued)

accomplish school tasks. The eight neurodevelopmental functions are

- Higher thinking
- Language
- Spatial ordering
- Sequential ordering
- Memory
- Attention
- Psychosocial/social thinking
- Motor coordination

Students must utilize these functions to varying degrees in order to succeed at different learning activities, including mathematical tasks. Each learner has a unique **neurodevelopmental profile**, a pattern of strengths and weaknesses in different neurodevelopmental functions. His or her profile can be more or less matched to the requirements or demands of different kinds of learning activities, which will influence his or her success at the task at hand. A learner's neurodevelopmental profile changes over time—each of his or her neurodevelopmental functions can grow in effectiveness, level off, or deteriorate. Many factors shape a learner's profile, including genetic factors, family factors, cultural values, environmental influences, educational experiences, physical health, peer influences, and emotional factors. Close observation and description of students' strengths and weaknesses are necessary to understand their neurodevelopmental profiles.

To effectively support individual students, teachers should aim for **management by profile**. This means taking into consideration individual students' strengths and weaknesses rather than focusing on isolated weak spots. Management by profile has multiple components. It involves **demystification** (helping students to understand their strengths and weaknesses), **accommodations** (building on students' strengths to bypass their weaknesses), and **interventions** at the breakdown points (strengthening a student's area of weakness). Teachers should take special care to strengthen students' strengths and affinities and to protect them from humiliation in an effort to nurture their sense of self-worth and efficacy.

children. The purpose of working in these teams is for teachers to benefit from each other's expertise and perspectives about their students.

Math for All places a strong emphasis on collaborative lesson planning, because we believe that making math lessons accessible to all students requires teachers to engage in an ongoing process of problem solving, decision making, and reflection. Often, there is not one single approach that will work for all students. Instead, teachers need to think about how the neurodevelopmental demands of a math lesson interact with individual students' strengths and needs, and carefully adapt and select materials, activities, and instructional strategies that are consistent with the original goal of the lesson and that help to make it accessible to students with various strengths and needs. Different students may need different types of support to reach the same goals. This does not mean that you need to create individual lesson plans for each student in your class. Instead, by focusing on a few students with different strengths and needs and planning adaptations based on their neurodevelopmental profiles, you will find that your lessons will become more accessible to many students in your classroom.

CONTENT AND FORMAT OF THE PROFESSIONAL DEVELOPMENT

In the morning of each workshop you will spend time examining videos and printed materials from a specific case lesson. Each workshop will focus on a different case lesson from different grade levels and with different math content (pre-algebra, data analysis, geometry, number and operations). You will work with the members of your team, applying parts of the lesson planning process to better understand how the case lessons were adapted. You will analyze the demands of the math activity of the case lesson, observe a focal child from the lesson engage in this activity to better understand his or her strengths and needs, review curriculum materials to understand the mathematical goals of the lesson, and examine the instructional strategies and teaching practices that the teacher in the case lesson uses to get a sense of how he or she adapted it to make it more accessible for the focal student and other students in the class.

In the second part of each workshop, you will have time to work with your team to apply what you learned earlier in the day while planning for a lesson that you will teach in between workshop sessions. The goal for your planning is to adapt the lesson to ensure that students with different strengths and needs in your classroom will be successful in meeting its goals. As with the case lesson, you will examine the math goals for your lesson, analyze its neurodevelopmental demands, consider the strengths and needs of one or more focal children, and select instructional strategies and teaching practices that will make the lesson accessible to the focal student(s) without changing the mathematical goals of the lesson.

You will leave each workshop with some assignments to complete before the next session. In addition to doing some reading, you will also be asked to work with the members of your team to carry out the adapted lesson and reflect on the success of the adaptations for your focal student(s) and other students in your classroom. You will be asked to share what you learned, and have an opportunity to find out what other teams have learned, at the following workshop. The assignments also offer opportunities for you and the facilitators of the professional development to have a private dialog around your work. The facilitators will give you feedback on your assignments. Reading about your experiences with implementing the adapted lessons in your classroom will help them to fine-tune the professional development based on your situation and needs.

The assignments are a key component of the *Math for All* program. They will allow you to apply what you learned to your classroom, and will allow your students to benefit from your professional development. You will have a chance to try out different approaches for making math accessible to all your students and to reflect on what works and what doesn't. This work is demanding, but you will be able to draw on the expertise and support of your colleagues and facilitators.

ONGOING LESSON PLANNING

We hope that the five workshops will allow you to experience enough of the results and benefits of the collaborative lesson planning process that you will continue to engage in it with your colleagues on an ongoing basis after the workshops end. Common prep times, grade level meetings, or faculty meetings may provide venues for doing so. While it is probably unlikely that you can collaboratively co-plan each and every lesson with a colleague, meeting with your team once a week or even once a month to work on a key lesson can make a big difference. In the appendices you will find copies of the lesson planning tools that you may duplicate to support you in your ongoing lesson planning. Ultimately, we hope that the process for planning accessible math lessons that *Math for All* is introducing you to will become a habit of mind that you will carry out in the natural course of your work.

Thank you for your commitment and efforts in improving the math education of all students!

Workshop 1

Planning Math Lessons That Reach All Learners

This workshop will introduce participants to a neurodevelopmental framework and a case lesson on pre-algebra. The case is a third-grade lesson in which students use interlocking cubes to determine the factors of a number and examine patterns in factor families. Participants will use the neurodevelopmental framework to explore the mathematical demands of the case lesson. You will use video to observe the work done by Jashandeep, a student who has difficulties with organizing her thoughts and her work on paper. You will also reflect on instructional strategies to support Jashandeep and other students in the classroom who have different strengths and needs.

Participants will select a focal child from their own classroom and work with the members of their team to plan for an observation of this child, which will be guided by the neurodevelopmental framework and carried out before the next workshop session. Participants will record their observations, reflect on them, and share their work at the beginning of Workshop 2.

You will:

1. Learn how to analyze the demands of a mathematical task using the neurodevelopmental framework.

2. Learn how to use the neurodevelopmental framework to guide their observation of students' strengths and needs.

3. Enhance their understanding of instructional strategies that support students with strengths and needs in different neurodevelopmental functions.

WORKSHOP 1   WORKSHEET 1A: WORKSHOP PARTICIPANT BINGO

Introduce yourself to your fellow workshop participants and find out who meets the descriptors below. If you find a person who meets one of the descriptors, write his or her name in that cell. Do not list the same person in more than one cell.

Has a new home	Likes chocolate	Is an auditory learner	Has two children	Likes to cook
Likes to travel	Has a cat	Likes to dance	Speaks another language	Has a dog
Has a brother	Likes to swim	Is an only child	Sings in a choir	Likes coffee
Has one child	Likes to ride a bicycle	Is a vegetarian	Is a tactile/ kinesthetic learner	Plays the guitar
Likes to play baseball	Plays the piano	Plays tennis	Likes to snowboard	Is a visual learner

Arranging 12 Cubes

① 1 tower or column
12 rows
1×12

② 2 towers or columns
6 rows
2×6

③ 4 columns
3 rows
4×3

④ 3 columns
4 rows
3×4

⑤ 6 columns
2 rows
6×2

⑥ 12 columns
1 row
12×1

What patterns do you notice about the number of columns and rows?

1.3

WORKSHOP 1   ADAPTED STUDENT WORKSHEET

Name(s): _____   Date: _____

Arranging Chairs

- ☐ 1. Explore one multiple. Find as many different arrangements as you can.
- ☐ 2. Record your arrangements/arrays with your partner.
- ☐ 3. What patterns are you and your partner noticing between the number of columns and rows?
- ☐ 4. How are the factors (or the number of columns and rows) changing?
- ☐ 5. Check your idea with another multiple. Does your pattern always work? (Use the bag or choose a multiple from 4 to 30)

Watch the video with the teacher's instructions for the activity. Carry out the activity with your group, following the teacher's instructions.

Observe and reflect on what skills you need to use to carry out this activity. Please use the space below to jot down your observations/reflections.

| WORKSHOP 1 | **WORKSHEET 1C: REACTIONS TO THE HANDS-ON EXPLORATION OF THE MATH ACTIVITY** |

Name: _____

Name of the Lesson: _____

Some things I found interesting when I carried out the activity myself:

1.

2.

3.

Some things I wouldn't have known about the activity if I hadn't explored it hands-on myself:

1.

2.

3.

Name of Activity or Lesson Explored: *Arranging Chairs*

Focal Student Name: *Jashandeep*

Learning Areas (Barringer, Pohlman, & Robinson, 2010; Levine, 2002; Pohlman,2008)	What roles do these learning areas play in the Arranging Chairs activity?	How does Jashandeep respond to the demands of the task? Please note strengths and needs below.	How did Cindy Wang change the Arranging Chairs activity and what teaching practices does she use to make it more accessible to Jashandeep? What additional change would you make?
Higher Thinking • using and forming concepts • solving problems • logical thinking • creative and critical thinking			
Language • understanding mathematical language • using language to communicate with others and to clarify one's ideas			

Spatial Ordering

- interpreting relationships within and between spatial patterns
- organizing things in space
- reasoning with images

Sequential Ordering

- organizing information in sequence
- following directions
- managing time

Memory

- short-term memory
- active working memory
- long-term memory

Attention

- controlling mental energy
- maintaining focus
- self-monitoring

Psychosocial

- using and understanding social language
- collaboration
- conflict resolution

Motor Coordination

- gross motor functions
- fine motor functions
- grapho-motor functions

WORKSHOP 1   **WORKSHEET 1E: LEARNING GOALS**

Your Name:_____   Focal Student Pseudonym:_____

Name of the Lesson: _____

Review the introductory pages for the unit of the Arranging Chairs lesson to help you answer the questions below. The unit overview is found on pages 17 (1.12) to 27 (1.22). The lesson guide is on pages 28 (1.23) to 35 (1.30).

1. What are the learning goals of the lesson?

2. In what ways do you think this lesson connects to what students have studied in math before (this school year and before)?

3. How do you think what students learn in this lesson will help them with the math they will learn in the future (this school year and beyond)?

WORKSHOP 1   WORKSHEET 1F: TEACHING PRACTICES

Think about your focal child (or another child from your classroom). Which of these teaching practices might work for him or her? How would you use these practices?

Teaching Practices	How would you use these practices with your focal student and other students in your classroom?
Use concept mapping.	
Model problem-solving steps and approaches.	
Model critical thinking steps and approaches.	
Have students record and/or represent the steps they went through to solve the problem or analyze an idea.	
Have students work in mixed-ability groups.	
Post a written or pictorial chart that shows the steps for solving problems or for critical thinking.	
Encourage students to model a problem using diagrams and manipulatives.	
Use problems that are relevant to students' experiences and interests.	
Allow and encourage the use of calculators.	
Use graphic organizers to help students organize information and detect patterns so that they can more readily come up with a rule.	

1.11

Unit Guide for "Arranging Chairs" Lesson

UNIT OVERVIEW

Things That Come in Groups

Content of This Unit   To develop experience with some uses of multiplication and division, students work with things that come in groups, with patterns in the multiplication tables using 100 charts, and with rectangular arrays. They invent and solve problems about the number of legs on living creatures. Students become familiar with the multiplication tables up to the 12's, with emphasis on multiples with totals under 50. They also invent their own ways of solving multiplication and division problems.

Connections with Other Units   If you are doing the full-year *Investigations* curriculum in the suggested sequence for grade 3, this is the second of 10 units. This unit introduces a variety of activities that use small numbers; these activities will be repeated later in *Landmarks in the Hundreds*, using larger numbers—with factors and multiples of 100.

This unit can be used successfully at either grade 3 or grade 4 as an introduction to multiplication and division, depending on the previous experience and needs of your students. Many of the ideas and games in this unit are picked up and extended in the grade 4 Multiplication and Division units.

Investigations Curriculum ■ Suggested Grade 3 Sequence

Mathematical Thinking at Grade 3 (Introduction)

▶ *Things That Come in Groups* (Multiplication and Division)

Flips, Turns, and Area (2-D Geometry)

From Paces to Feet (Measuring and Data)

Landmarks in the Hundreds (The Number System)

Up and Down the Number Line (Changes)

Combining and Comparing (Addition and Subtraction)

Turtle Paths (2-D Geometry)

Fair Shares (Fractions)

Exploring Solids and Boxes (3-D Geometry)

Investigation 1 ■ Things That Come in Groups		
Class Sessions	**Activities**	**Pacing**
Session 1 (p. 4) MANY THINGS COME IN GROUPS	Naming Things That Come in Groups Asking Multiplication Questions Brainstorming About Groups Homework: Things That Come in Groups	minimum 1 hr
Session 2 (p. 7) HOW MANY IN SEVERAL GROUPS?	Pictures of Things That Come in Groups Writing "Groups of" as Multiplication Homework: Pictures of Things That Come in Groups	minimum 1 hr
Session 3 (p. 12) WRITING AND SOLVING RIDDLES	Writing Riddles for Our Pictures Teacher Checkpoint: Do They Understand Multiplication? Homework: Riddled with Riddles!	minimum 1 hr
Session 4 (Excursion)* (p. 16) EACH ORANGE HAD 8 SLICES	How Many Altogether?	minimum 1 hr

◔ **Ten-Minute Math ■ Counting Around the Class**

*Excursions can be omitted without harming the integrity or continuity of the unit, but they offer good mathematical work if you have time to include them.

Mathematical Emphasis	**Assessment Resources**	**Materials**
■ Finding things that come in groups ■ Using multiplication notation ■ Using multiplication to mean groups of groups ■ Writing and illustrating multiplication sentences	What About Notation? (Teacher Note, p. 11) Teacher Checkpoint: Do They Understand Multiplication? (p. 14) The Relationship Between Division and Multiplication (Teacher Note, p. 15) How Many Petals? How Many Bugs? (Dialogue Box, p. 19)	Calculators Snap™ Cubes Art materials: paper; colored pencils, markers, or crayons Large paper *Each Orange Had 8 Slices* by Paul Giganti, Jr., and Donald Crews (opt.) Scissors Tape Student Sheets 1–3 Family letter

Investigation 2 ▪ Skip Counting and 100 Charts

Class Sessions	Activities	Pacing
Session 1 (p. 22) HIGHLIGHTING MULTIPLES IN 100 CHARTS	Highlighting 2's and 3's Making Books of 100 Charts Homework: Multiples on 100 Charts	minimum 1 hr
Session 2 (p. 26) USING THE CALCULATOR TO SKIP COUNT	Skip Counting 4's and More Homework: More Multiples on 100 Charts	minimum 1 hr
Sessions 3 and 4 (p. 28) MORE PRACTICE WITH MULTIPLES	Choice Time: Exploring Multiples and Patterns Teacher Checkpoint: Using the Skip Counting Circles Homework: Silly Story Problems Homework: Patterns Across the Charts	minimum 2 hr
Sessions 5 and 6 (p. 33) DISCUSSING NUMBER PATTERNS	Patterns in Multiples of 9 and 11 Numbers That Appear on Two Charts Discussion: Patterns Across the Charts Playing Cover 50 Homework: Cover 50 Game	minimum 2 hr

⏱ **Ten-Minute Math** ▪ **Counting Around the Class**

Mathematical Emphasis

▪ Recognizing that skip counting represents multiples of the same number and has a connection to multiplication

▪ Looking for patterns in multiples of 2 through 12 on the 100 chart

▪ Understanding that the patterns numbers make can help us multiply those numbers

Assessment Resources

Students' Problems with Skip Counting (Teacher Note, p. 25)

Teacher Checkpoint: Using the Skip Counting Circles (p. 31)

Multiples of 6 (Dialogue Box, p. 39)

Cover 50 (Dialogue Box, p. 39)

Materials

Overhead projector, transparencies, and transparency pens

Calculators

Snap™ Cubes

Art materials: colored pencils, markers, or crayons

Each Orange Had 8 Slices by Paul Giganti, Jr., and Donald Crews (opt.)

Envelopes or resealable plastic bags

Scissors

Stapler

Student Sheets 4–6

Teaching resource sheets

Investigation 3 ▪ Arrays and Skip Counting		
Class Sessions	**Activities**	**Pacing**
Sessions 1 and 2 (p. 42) ARRANGING CHAIRS	Arranging Chairs in Rectangular Arrays Arranging More Chairs Making Array Cards Homework: Cutting Out Array Cards	minimum 2 hr
Sessions 3 and 4 (p. 48) ARRAY GAMES	Counting Squares in Arrays Playing Array Games Homework: Array Games Extension: What Number Has the Most Arrays?	minimum 2 hr
Session 5 (p. 53) THE SHAPES OF ARRAYS	Discussing Array Game Strategies Assessment: Arrays That Total 36 Homework: More Array Games	minimum 1 hr
◷ Ten-Minute Math ▪ Counting Around the Class		

Mathematical Emphasis

- Recognizing that finding the area of a rectangle is one situation where multiplication can be used

- Using arrays to skip count

- Using arrays with skip counting to multiply and divide

- Finding factor pairs

- Making connections between number and shape

Assessment Resources

Arranging Chairs (Dialogue Box, p. 47)

Assessment: Arrays That Total 36 (Teacher Note, p. 55)

Materials

Overhead projector, transparencies, and pen

Calculators

Snap™ Cubes

Resealable plastic bags

Scissors

Array Cards

Student Sheet 7

Teaching resource sheets

WORKSHOP 1   LESSON MATERIALS

Investigation 4 ■ The Language of Multiplication and Division

Class Sessions	Activities	Pacing
Sessions 1 and 2 (p. 58) MULTIPLY OR DIVIDE?	Solving Story Problems Acting Out Number Sentences Different Ways to Write Problems Writing Multiplication and Division Sentences Teacher Checkpoint: Do They Understand the Notation? Homework: More Story Problems Homework: Decribe the Problem Extension: Interpreting Problems on Standardized Tests	minimum 2 hr
Sessions 3 and 4 (p. 70) WRITING AND SOLVING STORY PROBLEMS	Writing Story Problems A Class Book of Problems Solving Problems in the Class Book Homework: The Class Book at Home Extension: Problems About the Class	minimum 2 hr

🕐 Ten-Minute Math ■ Likely or Unlikely?

Mathematical Emphasis	Assessment Resources	Materials
■ Understanding relationships between multiplication and division ■ Identifying whether word problems can be solved using division and/or multiplication ■ Using multiplication and division notation to write number sentences	Teacher Checkpoint: Do They Understand the Notation? (p. 66) Talking and Writing About Division (Teacher Note, p. 67) Would You Use Multiplication or Division? (Dialogue Box, p. 68) Two Kinds of Division: Sharing and Partitioning (Teacher Note, p. 68)	Overhead projector, transparencies, and pen Calculators Snap™ Cubes Art materials: colored paper; plain paper; colored pencils, markers, or crayons Chart paper and marker Stapler Student Sheets 8–11 Teaching resource sheets

I-16 ■ *Things That Come in Groups*

Investigation 5 ▪ Problems with Larger Numbers

Class Sessions	Activities	Pacing
Session 1 (p. 76) CALCULATING SAVINGS	How Much Would You Save? Homework: How Much Would You Save? Extension: How Many Months Old Are You?	minimum 1 hr
Session 2 (p. 79) MANY, MANY LEGS	Discussion: What Could We Buy? How Many Legs? Planning a Survey Homework: Creatures in Our Homes and Neighborhoods	minimum 1 hr
Session 3 (p. 83) DATA TABLES AND LINE PLOTS	Expanding Our Data Tables Making a Line Plot Problems from Our Own Data Homework: Finishing Display Pages	minimum 1 hr
Session 4 (p. 87) A RIDDLE WITH 22 LEGS	Assessment: A Riddle with 22 Legs Choosing Student Work to Save	minimum 1 hr

🕐 Ten-Minute Math ▪ Likely or Unlikely?

Mathematical Emphasis

- Multiplying and dividing in real-life situations and using patterns to solve multiplication and division problems

- Organizing and presenting data in tables and line plots

- Sorting out complex problems that require both multiplication and addition

- Making up division and multiplication story problems from real data

Assessment Resources

Assessment: A Riddle with 22 Legs (p. 87)

Choosing Student Work to Save (p. 89)

Materials

Overhead projector, transparencies, and pen

Calculators

Art materials: drawing paper; colored pencils, markers, or crayons

Student Sheets 12–15

Teaching resource sheets

WORKSHOP 1   LESSON MATERIALS

MATERIALS LIST

Following are the basic materials needed for the activities in this unit.

- Snap™ Cubes (interlocking cubes): 50 per student

- Array Cards (manufactured, or use blackline masters at the back of this book to make your own sets). Cutting out Array Cards can take students a great deal of time. If you use the blackline masters, enlist the help of classroom aides to cut out (but not label) sets of cards for your students to use in class. Since students will need a set for homework, they can also take a set home to cut out with the help of family members. Array Cards are introduced in Investigation 3.

- Calculators: at least 1 per pair of students

- *Each Orange Had 8 Slices* by Paul Giganti, Jr., and Donald Crews (optional)

- Scissors: 1 per student

- Legal-size envelopes

- Quart-size resealable plastic bags

- Large paper for making class lists

- Colored paper, drawing paper

- Colored pencils, markers, or crayons

- Overhead projector

- Blank overhead transparencies, pens

- Scissors

- Stapler

- Chart paper, marker

The following materials are provided at the end of this unit as blackline masters. A Student Activity Booklet containing all student sheets and teacher resources needed for individual work is available.

Family Letter (p. 98)
Student Sheets 1–15 (p. 99)
Teaching Resources:
    Cover 50 Game (p. 105)
    How to Play Cover 50 (p. 106)
    Array Cards (p. 108)
    How to Make Array Cards (p. 114)
    The Arranging Chairs Puzzle (p. 115)
    How to Play Multiplication Pairs (p. 116)
    How to Play Count and Compare (p. 117)
    Number Problems (p. 122)
    Half-Inch Graph Paper (p. 127)
Practice Pages (p. 129)

Related Children's Literature

Axelrod, Amy. *Pigs Will Be Pigs*. New York: Four Winds Press, 1994.

Carle, Eric. *The Very Hungry Caterpillar*. New York: World Publishing, 1969.

Giganti, Paul, Jr., and Donald Crews. *Each Orange Had 8 Slices*. New York: Greenwillow, 1992.

Low, Joseph. *Mice Twice*. New York: Atheneum, 1980.

I-18 ▪ *Things That Come in Groups*

Note: The blackline masters for this unit are not included in this book.

ABOUT THE MATHEMATICS IN THIS UNIT

In this unit, students develop their own strategies for doing multiplication and division problems. They discover that both types of problems deal with equal groups, but each will answer different questions about the groups. Multiplication is typically used when the size of each group and the number of groups is known, and we want to find the total number of items. Division is most often used when the total quantity is known, and we want to find out either the number or the size of the groups.

As students develop strategies to use in multiplication and division situations, it is critical that they develop visual images that support their work. They may use an array of squares, for example, to visualize an important multiplication relationship—that the solution to 7×6 is the same as the solution to 6×7. As students skip count on a 100 chart, they begin to recognize characteristics of particular multiples. They will see, for example, that all the multiples of 2, 4, and 6 are even numbers, or that all the multiples of 5 end in either 5 or 0. Students may at first visualize multiplication as repeated addition, since this process is more familiar to them.

Throughout this unit, it is most important to support students' efforts to make sense out of multiplication and division. As students develop their own strategies, they are aided by knowing many of the single-digit multiplication pairs. We do not expect them to memorize all the multiples, but as they look at patterns in the tables and construct the multiples again and again by skip counting, students will commit many of them to memory. They will also pick up ways to solve others quickly—for example, by using a known answer to find an unknown one ("8×6 is like 4×6 twice, so it's 24 and 24, and that's 48").

Students also learn to read standard multiplication and division notation and to use this notation to record their work. They must also learn that notation communicates the problem to be solved but doesn't prescribe the method of solution.

When students see problems written in standard forms such as these:

$$\begin{array}{r} 56 \\ \times\,8 \\ \hline \end{array} \qquad 4\overline{)132}$$

the form of the problem may trigger use of poorly understood, and often inefficient, algorithms. For example, in the first problem, students might start to say, "8 times 6 is 48, put down the 8 and carry the 4…." This procedure obscures the use of good number sense and often leads students to fragment a number into its digits and lose track of the quantities represented by the numerals. Good mental strategies often start from the left, focusing first on the largest part of the number, rather than the smallest: "eight 50's is 400, eight 6's is 48, so that's 448."

Students need to develop efficient computation strategies, many of which will be mental strategies, but these must be based on their understanding of the quantities and their relationships, not on memorized procedures. We would like students to recognize multiplication and division problems written in all of the notations they are likely to see in elementary school but to solve them in their own way.

At the beginning of each investigation, the Mathematical Emphasis section tells you what is most important for students to learn about during that investigation. Many of these mathematical understandings are difficult and complex. Students gradually learn more and more about each idea over many years of schooling. Individual students will begin and end the unit with different levels of knowledge and skill, but all will gain greater knowledge about multiples and factors and about some meanings and notation for multiplication and division.

ABOUT THE ASSESSMENT IN THIS UNIT

Throughout the *Investigations* curriculum, there are many opportunities for ongoing daily assessment as you observe, listen to, and interact with students at work. In this unit, you will find three Teacher Checkpoints:

Investigation 1, Session 3:
Do They Understand Multiplication? (p. 14)

Investigation 2, Sessions 3–4:
Using the Skip Counting Circles (p. 31)

Investigation 4, Sessions 1–2:
Do They Understand the Notation? (p. 66)

This unit also has two embedded Assessment activities:

Investigation 3, Session 5:
Arrays That Total 36 (p. 54)

Investigation 5, Session 4:
A Riddle with 22 Legs (p. 87)

In addition, you can use almost any activity in this unit to assess your students' needs and strengths. Listed below are questions to help you focus your observations in each investigation. You may want to keep track of your observations for each student to help you plan your curriculum and monitor students' growth. Suggestions for documenting student growth can be found in the section About Assessment.

Investigation 1: Things That Come in Groups

- How easily do students generate ideas of items that come in groups? Where do they look for ideas? (For example, do they check around the classroom? Around school? At home? At a store?)

- How do students write number sentences when describing groups of objects? How do they interpret standard notation? How do they solve problems presented in standard notation?

- How do children show that they understand the structure of multiplication problems? How do they explain the meaning of a multiplication equation? Do they talk about groups?

- How do children write and interpret multiplication sentences? How do they draw an illustration to represent a multiplication sentence? Do they understand the connection between the sentence and the illustration?

Investigation 2: Skip Counting and 100 Charts

- How do students skip count during various activities? What numbers do they seem most comfortable skip counting with? How do they use skip counting and the 100 chart to solve multiplication problems? What language do students use to discuss factors and multiples?

- What patterns do students notice about the numbers that are (and are not) highlighted on their multiple charts? What kinds of observations do they make? Do they investigate the behavior of odd and even numbers on the multiple charts?

- How do students use their 100 charts (and the patterns on them) to help them solve multiplication problems? What do students notice when overheads of two different factors of a multiple are overlaid? What predictions do they make about other multiples on the basis of this knowledge?

Investigation 3: Arrays and Skip Counting

- How do students find the total number of squares in an array? Do they see this as a multiplication situation? How do they use multiplication?

- When figuring the total of an array, how do the students count the squares that make up that array? Do they count by 1's, or do they skip count by the number in a row or column?

- How do students find one dimension of an array when they have the second dimension and the total number of squares?

- How do students go about finding all possible dimensions for array shapes? How do they use their knowledge of one factor pair to influence their choice of another (for example, 2×4 is the same as 4×2)? Are they organized and systematic in their approach?

- How do students identify the dimensions of an array when they know only the total number of squares in that array? How do they use what they know about relationships between shape and number?

Investigation 4: The Language of Multiplication and Division

- How do students express multiplication problems as division problems? How do they use related problems of the opposite operation to help them?

- How do children interpret word problems? How do they decide whether to use multiplication or division?

- How do children use notation to write the number sentences for word problems? How many types of notation do they use? Do their equations match the question the word problem is asking?

Investigation 5: Problems with Larger Numbers

- What methods do students use to multiply or divide in real-life situations? Do they use known patterns?

- How do students organize data? Are their representations clear? Can you gather information from them? How do they clarify their representations when someone has a question?

- How do children make sense of and solve problems involving both multiplication and addition? How do they organize and keep track of their work?

- How do students make up story problems from real data? What variables do children include? How do they make them challenging?

Assessment Sourcebook

In the *Assessment Sourcebook* you will find End-of-Unit Assessment Tasks and Assessment Masters available in English and Spanish. You will also find suggestions to help you observe and evaluate student work and checklists of mathematical emphases with space for you to record individual student information.

WORKSHOP 1   **LESSON MATERIALS**

PREVIEW FOR THE LINGUISTICALLY DIVERSE CLASSROOM

In the *Investigations* curriculum, mathematical vocabulary is introduced naturally during the activities. We don't ask students to learn definitions of new terms; rather, they come to understand such words as *factor* or *area* or *symmetry* by hearing them used frequently in discussion as they investigate new concepts. This approach is compatible with current theories of second-language acquisition, which emphasize the use of new vocabulary in meaningful contexts while students are actively involved with objects, pictures, and physical movement.

Listed below are some key words used in this unit that will not be new to most English speakers at this age level, but may be unfamiliar to students with limited English proficiency. You will want to spend additional time working on these words with your students who are learning English. If your students are working with a second-language teacher, you might enlist your colleague's aid in familiarizing students with these words, before and during this unit. In the classroom, look for opportunities for students to hear and use these words. Activities you can use to present the words are given in the appendix, Vocabulary Support for Second-Language Learners (p. 95).

question, statement, illustrate In Investigation 1, students write and *illustrate* their own multiplication "riddles," making two or more *statements* involving numbers, and ending with a *question*.

chart, row, column Students color in multiples on the 100 *chart* in Investigation 2, looking for visual patterns in its *rows* and *columns*, as well as diagonals.

calculator, press, equals key, plus key Students learn to use the calculator to skip count by any number, *pressing* that number, the *plus key*, and then the *equals key* repeatedly.

day, week, month, amount In a savings problem in Investigation 5, students find the *amount* of money they would save in a *week* or a *month* by saving the same amount each *day*.

creature, leg, -legged In a series of activities during Investigation 5 that involve working with larger numbers, students investigate various combinations of creatures with different numbers of legs.

Multicultural Extensions for All Students
Whenever possible, encourage students to share words, objects, customs, or any aspects of daily life from their own cultures and backgrounds that are relevant to the activities in this unit. For example:

- When students are thinking of things that come in groups during the first investigation, encourage them to include groups of things that may reflect their culture—such as the number of dancers in a particular dance, or the number of playing pieces in a popular game.

- When students are writing story problems in Investigation 4, encourage the use of culture-specific references (to items of food, for example) so that in sharing their problems with the class, they share a little of themselves as well.

I-22 ▪ *Things That Come in Groups*

From *Investigations, Grade Level 3, Things That Come in Groups,* by Cornelia Tierney, Mary Berle-Carman, & Joan Akers. Copyright by Pearson Education, Inc., or its affiliate(s). Used by permission. All rights reserved.

Note: The appendix "Vocabulary Support for Second-Language Learners" is not included in this book.

INVESTIGATION 3

Arrays and Skip Counting

What Happens

Sessions 1 and 2: Arranging Chairs Challenged to find different ways to arrange rows of chairs for an audience, students manipulate 12 cubes to see how many different rectangles they can make. They list the dimensions of these rectangles and the factors of 12. Students work individually and in pairs to determine the factors of other numbers by making rectangles. They also begin making sets of array cards for use throughout the investigation.

Sessions 3 and 4: Array Games Students talk about ways to count the total in arrays, and they learn two array games—Multiplication Pairs, and Count and Compare. In addition, students can choose to do further work on the Arranging Chairs puzzle. These activities give students practice multiplying and dividing and encourage them to develop connections between number and shape.

Session 5: The Shapes of Arrays Students briefly discuss strategies for working with arrays. Then they do an assessment problem that involves identifying by shape the arrays with a total of 36 and identifying the factors of 36. Students continue to play array games, if time permits.

Mathematical Emphasis

- Recognizing that finding the area of a rectangle is one situation where multiplication can be used
- Using arrays to skip count
- Using arrays with skip counting to multiply and divide
- Finding factor pairs
- Making connections between number and shape

40 ■ *Investigation 3: Arrays and Skip Counting*

WORKSHOP 1   **LESSON GUIDE FOR "ARRANGING CHAIRS" LESSON**

INVESTIGATION 3

What to Plan Ahead of Time

Materials

- Overhead projector and transparency pen (Sessions 1–4)
- Interlocking cubes: at least 30 per student (Sessions 1–2, 5)
- Calculators: 1 per pair (Sessions 1–2)
- Quart-size resealable plastic bags to hold Array Cards: 1 per student (Sessions 1–2)
- Scissors: 1 per student (Sessions 1–2)
- Array Cards (Sessions 1–4). If you do not have manufactured cards, make your own; see Other Preparation.

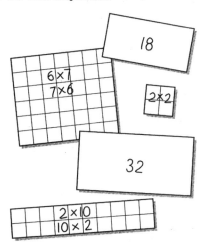

Other Preparation

- Duplicate student sheets and teaching resources (located at the end of this unit)

in the following quantities. If you have Student Activity Booklets, copy only the item marked with an asterisk.

For Sessions 1–2
Half-inch graph paper (p. 127): 2–3 sheets per student (optional), 1 transparency* (optional)
Array sheets 1–6 (p. 108): 1 set per student (homework)
How to Make Array Cards (p. 114): 1 per student (homework)

For Sessions 3–4
The Arranging Chairs Puzzle (p. 115): 1 per student (homework)
How to Play Multiplication Pairs (p. 116): 1 per student (homework)
How to Play Count and Compare (p. 117): 1 per student (homework)

For Session 5
Student Sheet 7, Arrays That Total 36 (p. 107): 1 per student

- If you do not have manufactured Array Cards for *Investigations* grade 3, use the blackline masters at the back of this book to make 1 set of cards per student for class use. (See What to Plan Ahead of Time for Investigation 1.) Students make another set for homework use. (Sessions 1–2)
- Make overhead transparencies of the Array Cards. Cut apart the 51 arrays, which represent the multiplication combinations of the factors 2 through 12 with totals up to 50. Do not label the dimensions or the total. (Sessions 3–4)

Investigation 3: Arrays and Skip Counting ■ **41**

Note: The student sheets, teaching resources, and blackline masters for this unit are not included in this book.

Sessions 1 and 2

Arranging Chairs

Materials

- Overhead projector, transparency pen
- Interlocking cubes (30 per student)
- Calculators (1 per pair)
- Half-inch graph paper (2–3 sheets per student, 1 transparency) (optional)
- Array Card pages (1 set per student, homework)
- Scissors (1 per student)
- Quart-size resealable plastic bags (1 per student)
- How to Make Array Cards (1 per student, homework)

What Happens

Challenged to find different ways to arrange rows of chairs for an audience, students manipulate 12 cubes to see how many different rectangles they can make. They list the dimensions of these rectangles and the factors of 12. Students work individually and in pairs to determine the factors of other numbers by making rectangles. They also begin making sets of Array Cards for use throughout the investigation. Their work focuses on:

- making rectangles for quantities of 12 and other numbers
- finding factors of 12 and other numbers

Ten-Minute Math: Counting Around the Class Continue to do Counting Around the Class two or three times during this investigation. Remember that this activity is intended to be done outside of math time.

Count by numbers whose patterns are now reasonably familiar to your students: 2's, 5's, 10's, and perhaps 3's, 4's, or 9's. Students can refer to their highlighted charts if they wish.

Ask students to predict ahead. For example, for counting by 3's, ask questions like these:

Who will say 15? Who will say 21? Khanh will be the twelfth student. What number will he say? What number will the student after Khanh say?

Ask questions about how high the counting will go.

Will we reach 50? 100? 200? What do you think will be our final number?

For full instructions and variations on this activity, see p. 91.

Activity

Arranging Chairs in Rectangular Arrays

Introducing Arrays   Each student needs 12 cubes to work with. Put 12 cubes on the overhead projector. Briefly explain the task:

Here's a puzzle to solve. We'll call it the Arranging Chairs puzzle. Pretend these 12 cubes are chairs. You want to arrange them in straight rows for an audience to watch a class play. You need to arrange the chairs so that there will be the same number in every row. How many different ways could you do this? How many chairs would be in each row? How many rows would there be? Try many different ways to arrange the chairs, even if some ways seem a bit silly for watching a class play.

❖   **Tip for the Linguistically Diverse Classroom**   To support your explanation of the task, model the arranging of four chairs in different ways—one row of 4 across, four rows of 1 (one behind another), and two rows of 2. Make the corresponding arrangement of cubes for each.

Students spend some time making as many different rectangles as they can using the 12 cubes. When they have made several possible arrays, ask them to identify the number of rows and the number of chairs in each row. Show the students' different rectangles by drawing them on an overhead transparency of graph paper, on large graph paper, or on the board. Label the dimensions on each array that you show.

Sessions 1 and 2: Arranging Chairs ▪ **43**

Identify for students the words *array* and *dimension*.

Mathematicians sometimes call things that are grouped this way to form a rectangle an *array*.

Dimension **is a name for the length or width of a rectangle. What are the** *dimensions* **of your rectangles? See how I'm labeling the dimensions of the rectangles as I draw them, the** *length* **and the** *width*.

Use the term *by* when talking about dimensions and students will copy you; for example, "The dimensions of this rectangle are 2 *by* 6." List the pairs of dimensions on the board.

$$3 \times 4 \qquad 2 \times 6 \qquad 1 \times 12$$
$$4 \times 3 \qquad 6 \times 2 \qquad 12 \times 1$$

Have we made all of the possible rectangles? Is our list of dimensions complete? Each of the dimensions on this list is a *factor* **of 12. What are all the factors of 12? (1, 2, 3, 4, 6, 12)**

Activity

Arranging More Chairs

Students continue to work on the Arranging Chairs puzzle, this time with different numbers of chairs. Give each pair of students one of the following numbers to work with:

| 15 | 16 | 18 | 19 | 20 | 21 | 24 | 25 | 30 |

You might assign the numbers or conduct a drawing. If each pair does more than one number (so that all numbers are done by at least two pairs), different pairs who are working on the same number can compare their answers.

The pairs use cubes to make different arrays of chairs for their number. Then they make drawings of all the arrays they find. If you want, supply half-inch graph paper to make drawing the arrays easier. For each number they work with, students make a list of dimension pairs titled "All the Ways of Arranging ___ Chairs." They may use calculators to find or check the dimensions of their arrays.

See the **Dialogue Box**, Arranging Chairs (p. 47), for an example of a student pair trying to find all possible arrangements of 15 chairs.

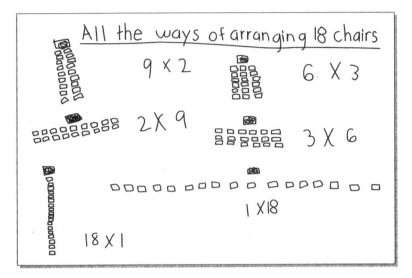

When they are finished, invite pairs of students to report their findings, one number at a time. Make a list of the dimensions of the arrays students made for each number. Point out that the number 19 makes only two arrays—1 by 19, and 19 by 1. Remind students about prime numbers— those that didn't turn up on any highlighted charts except their own. Ask:

What other numbers would have only two arrays?

<hr>

Activity

Making Array Cards

The six pages of Array Cards provide 51 arrays—every possible array representing the multiplication equations in the 2 to 12 tables *with totals up to 50.* If you have purchased the grade 3 manufactured materials for the *Investigations* curriculum, you will have printed sets of these 51 Array Cards that students can use in class. If not, you or an aide will have already made sets of cards for class use. In either case, each student will also benefit from making an individual set of paper Array Cards to use for homework assignments.

Give each student a set of Array Card pages, scissors, and a quart-size resealable plastic bag to hold the cut-apart array cards. Introduce the process of cutting out and labeling the cards as a whole-class activity. Give students time to practice with one or two sheets, and then have them do the rest as homework. Emphasize that all the cards will need to be prepared before the next session. (Some teachers use this student-made set for both homework and classwork. In that case, underscore the importance of preparing and returning the cards to school for the next session.)

Sessions 1 and 2: Arranging Chairs ▪ **45**

Explain the procedure:

1. Start with Array Cards, page 1. The students are to carefully cut out each individual array on the sheet, following the outlines of the grid as exactly as possible. (Seeing the exact outline of each array is important for the array games they will be playing.)

2. Students then label the grid side of each card with the dimensions of the grid.

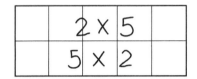

3. On the other side of each card (the blank side), students are to write the total number of squares in the grid. They may find it helpful to check the totals with a classmate or with someone at home before they write it permanently. Students may also write one of the dimensions of the grid on the total side, very lightly in pencil, to help them when the arrays are new. These can be erased when the students feel more confident.

4. Students write their initials on each card (in a corner away from the numbers) and store the labeled cards in the plastic bag.

Before students work independently, you might have them make some of the larger arrays. As students are working, walk around the room and observe whether they understand what to do and how each card should be prepared.

Sessions 1 and 2 Follow-Up

 **Homework**

Cutting Out Array Cards   For homework, students finish cutting out the Array Cards that they began making in class. Be sure to send home, besides the Array Card sheets, the plastic storage bags and copies of the sheet How to Make Array Cards as a reminder of how the cards are to be labeled. If this is their classroom set, emphasize that students are to bring their bags of cards back to class with them tomorrow. If this is a set to keep at home, remind students to store their bags of cards in a safe place.

D I A L O G U E   B O X

Arranging Chairs

Ricardo and Kate are working to find all the different ways to arrange 15 "chairs" for the Arranging Chairs puzzle. They have made 3 rows of 5, 5 rows of 3, 1 row of 15, and 15 rows of 1, as their drawing shows. They are now considering whether they have all the possibilities.

Is that all there is for 15 chairs?

Kate: I think so.

How can you find out?

Ricardo: From experimenting, but nothing is even any more.

What does that have to do with it?

Ricardo: I could do like 14. Let's see, 7 + 7 is 14, so 7 + 8 ... but that wouldn't be even rows, so it has to be two odds or something.

What do you know about two odds?

Kate: They make an even.

Ricardo: So, if we're missing any, it has to be odd + even. 1 + 2 doesn't work. 1 + 3 doesn't. I guess *none* of those work, because that wouldn't ever be even rows.

You see how you're starting at the beginning and making an organized list? [*Ricardo nods.*] **Well, that's what mathematicians do when they want to see if they've found all the possibilities.**

Ricardo: You're kidding!

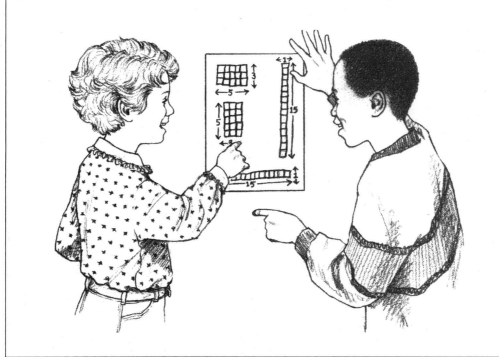

Sessions 1 and 2: Arranging Chairs ▪ **47**

Name(s): Jashandeep Siddicge   Date: 1/8/06

Arranging Chairs

☐ 1. Explore one multiple. Find as many different arrangements as you can.

☐ 2. Record your arrangements/arrays with your partner.

☐ 3. What patterns are you and your partner noticing between the number of columns and rows?

☐ 4. How are the factors (or the number of columns and rows) changing?

☐ 5. Check your idea with another multiple. Does your pattern always work? (Use the bag or choose a multiple from 4 to 30)

$1 \times 24 = 24$

$8 \times 3 = 24$

8 towers

8 colmens

$2 \times 12 = 24$

$12 \times 2 = 24$

$3 \times 8 = 24$ $6 \times 4 = 24$

But when you have an odd or even you along could break number's that are even not odd.

Name(s): David   Taren   Date: _____

Arranging Chairs

☐ 1. Explore one multiple. Find as many different arrangements as you can.

☐ 2. Record your arrangements/arrays with your partner.

☐ 3. What patterns are you and your partner noticing between the number of columns and rows?

☐ 4. How are the factors (or the number of columns and rows) changing?

☐ 5. Check your idea with another multiple. Does your pattern always work? (Use the bag or choose a multiple from 4 to 30)

$$\overset{\text{column row}}{1 \times 24} = 24$$
$$2 \times 12 = 24$$

arrows
12 colmaus

12 rows
2 colmaus $12 \times 2 = 24$

4 rows
6 colmaus $4 \times 6 = 24$

1 row
24 colmaus $1 \times 24 = 24$

4 rows $4 \times 6 = 24$

6 colmaus
6 rows $6 \times 4 = 24$
4 colmaus

1.32

Name(s): Rahul, Edgar, Harpreet   Date: 1/18/06

Arranging Chairs

☑ 1. Explore one multiple. Find as many different arrangements as you can.

☐ 2. Record your arrangements/arrays with your partner.

☐ 3. What patterns are you and your partner noticing between the number of columns and rows?

☐ 4. How are the factors (or the number of columns and rows) changing?

☐ 5. Check your idea with another multiple. Does your pattern always work? (Use the bag or choose a multiple from 4 to 30)

$$8 \times 5 = 40$$

$$1 \times 40 = 40$$

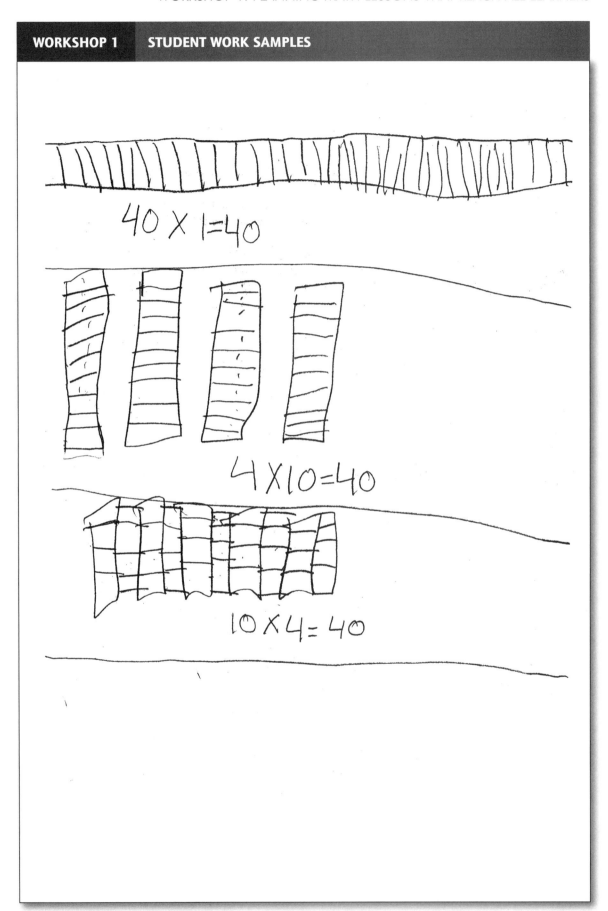

40 X 1 = 40

4 X 10 = 40

10 X 4 = 40

In preparation for the next Math for All Workshop, please complete the following assignments:

1. Conduct an observation of your focal child during a math lesson. Please follow the instructions below and use the Lesson Planning Chart to note the child's strengths and needs. After you have completed the observation, please answer the reflection questions.

2. Make sure to bring the completed Lesson Planning Chart and your answers to the reflection questions to the next workshop session. The facilitators may ask you to share your observations and will collect your charts and reflections so they can learn more about the children in your classrooms and your thinking about them. Feel free to submit the Demands of the Task and Observation Charts *as a group* if you worked on them together. However, please answer and submit the Reflection Questions *individually*.

3. Please read one of the following selections:

   • Chapters 2 ("Bringing the Science of Learning into the Classroom") and 3 ("Key Ingredients of Learning") from *Schools for All Kinds of Minds* (Barringer, Pohlman, & Robinson, 2010).

   • Chapters 2 ("The Ways of Learning") and 11 ("Getting a Mind Realigned") from *A Mind at a Time* (Levine, 2002).

4. Bring the textbooks and/or other curriculum materials you will be using between Workshop 2 and Workshop 3 to the next workshop session. You will need to use the books during the workshop to do some planning for a lesson that you will be teaching between the second and third workshop session.

PREPARING FOR AND CONDUCTING YOUR OBSERVATION OF A CHILD

1. Together with the members of your team, select a math lesson that you will teach over the next few weeks in which you can observe your focal child.

2. Read the description of the lesson and enact it with your colleagues (actually do the work of the lesson; don't just think about how it will be done). With your team, analyze the demands of the lesson, or a specific task within that lesson. Write down your conclusions in the second column of the Demands of the Task chart.

3. Conduct a 10- to 15-minute observation of your focal child in the lesson you selected. Take notes on the observation chart. Make sure to note both strengths and needs.

4. Answer the Reflection Questions.

WORKSHOP 1	DEMANDS OF THE TASK CHART

Your Name: _____ When Lesson Will Be Taught: _____

Name of Activity or Lesson Explored: _____

Learning Areas (based on Barringer et al., 2010; Levine, 2002; Pohlman, 2008)	What role do these learning areas play in the lesson?
Higher Thinking • using and forming concepts • solving problems • logical thinking • creative and critical thinking	
Language • understanding mathematical language • using language to communicate with others and to clarify one's ideas	
Spatial Ordering • interpreting relationships within and between spatial patterns • storing and recalling shapes, symbols, imagery, and appearances • organizing things in space (physical tools, workspace, information/data) • reasoning and conceptualizing with images	
Sequential Ordering • organizing information in sequence • following directions • managing time	

1.36

Memory • short-term memory • active working memory • long-term memory	
Attention • controlling mental energy • maintaining focus • self-monitoring	
Psychosocial • using and understanding social language • collaboration • conflict resolution	
Motor Coordination • gross motor functions • fine motor functions • grapho-motor functions	

WORKSHOP 1	OBSERVATION CHART

Your Name: _____ Focal Student Pseudonym: _____

Name of Activity or Lesson Explored: _____

Learning Areas (based on Barringer et al., 2010; Levine, 2002; Pohlman, 2008)	How did the focal student respond to the various demands of the activity or lesson? Please note strengths and needs below
Higher Thinking • using and forming concepts • solving problems • logical thinking • creative and critical thinking	
Language • understanding mathematical language • using language to communicate with others and to clarify one's ideas	
Spatial Ordering • interpreting relationships within and between spatial patterns • storing and recalling shapes, symbols, imagery, and appearances • organizing things in space (physical tools, workspace, information/data) • reasoning and conceptualizing with images	
Sequential Ordering • organizing information in sequence • following directions • managing time	
Memory • short-term memory • active working memory • long-term memory	

Attention • controlling mental energy • maintaining focus • self-monitoring	
Psychosocial • using and understanding social language • collaboration • conflict resolution	
Motor Coordination • gross motor functions • fine motor functions • grapho-motor functions	

WORKSHOP 1 | **WORKSHEET 1G: LEARNING GOALS**

Your Name: _____ When Lesson Will Be Taught: _____

Focal Student Pseudonym: _____

Name of the Lesson: _____

Review the introductory pages for the unit of the Arranging Chairs lesson to help you answer the questions below. The unit overview is found on pages 17 (1.12) to 27 (1.22). The lesson guide is on pages 28 (1.23) to 35 (1.30).

1. What are the learning goals of the lesson?

2. In what ways do you think this lesson connects to what students have studied in math before (this school year and before)?

3. How do you think what students learn in this lesson will help them with the math they will learn in the future (this school year and beyond)?

1.40

WORKSHOP 1	REFLECTION QUESTIONS

Your Name: _____ Focal Student Pseudonym: _____

1. In what ways did your hands-on exploration and analysis of the lesson/math activity help you think about its demands? Did you learn anything new about the lesson/activity? Please explain.

2. How did observing a child enhance your understanding of how the child learns and his or her strengths and needs?

3. What things were hard about your assignment (conducting an observation of a child)?

4. What are the implications of what you learned about this child for your work with this child and other students in your class?

Workshop 2

Supporting Language Functions

In this workshop we will focus in depth on one of the neurodevelopmental functions, language use and communication. You will explore the role of language in learning mathematics and learn about different components of language functions. Participants will use video and other materials from a fourth-grade case lesson on data analysis to analyze the language demands of the focal task, which involves gathering numerical data and representing it. You will also observe Ariel, an English language learner who is easily distracted, to assess his strengths and needs in language functions. Using video of the case lesson's teacher as a springboard, participants will consider instructional strategies that will support the language functions of Ariel as well as other students in this lesson.

You will work in teams to select a lesson that you will teach before the next workshop to plan language adaptations for a focal child. You will analyze the goals and language demands of the lesson, think about their focal child's strengths and needs in language functions, and plan for adaptations to help ensure that your focal child will be able to meet the learning goals of the lesson. Participants will record and reflect on the implementation of their adaptations and share your experiences at the beginning of Workshop 3.

You will

1. Deepen your understanding of the many uses of language in mathematics.

2. Learn how to analyze the language demands of a mathematical task.

3. Learn how to use the neurodevelopmental framework to assess with student's strengths and needs in relation to using language in math.

4. Broaden your understanding of specific instructional strategies for supporting language use in math.

5. Learn to use your analyses of the neurodevelopmental demands of the task and the strengths and needs of their students to guide planning of adaptations for their math lessons.

How Many Raisins in a Box?

Name_____   Date_____

INSTRUCTIONS: Count your *raisins*. Then **ask your partner** the **questions** below.

REMEMBER! <u>DO NOT</u> EAT THE RAISINS!..(At least, not until later!)

QUESTIONS
Answer these YES or NO questions.   CIRCLE ONE

1. Did you count your raisins by 1s?   Y   N
2. Did you count your raisins in multiples of 5s?   Y   N
3. Did you count your raisins in multiples of 10s?   Y   N
4. If you did NOT count in multiples of 1s, 5s, or 10s, *how* did you count?
   EXPLAIN your partners strategy in the space below.

5. How many *raisins* were in your box? _____raisins
   a. **Please use one of the markers at your table to WRITE** *your partner's number* **on a Post-It.**
   b. **Write in BIG NUMBERS so we can see your number from far away.**
   c. **Place the Post-It on the board.**

If you have time

At the rug, we collected data about how many people had dogs, brown eyes, and blue jeans? We also found out how many people take the bus to school.

What other data can you collect? What information would you like to find out about your class? *Make a list of questions in the table below.* (I started the table out for you.)

Data I can find out by counting	1. How many people in the class like *chocolate* ice cream? 2.
Data I can find out by measuring	
Data I can find out by conducting experiments	

2.2

Names of group members: _____ & _____   Date _____

OUR CLASS DATA:
How many raisins are in the box?

INSTRUCTIONS: *Find a way to organize the data we collected. Use the data from the class Post-its.*
Make a rough draft sketch. (You will only have 10 minutes to do this.)

What do you notice about your data? Write down three important things you can say about the data.

1.

2.

3.

Watch the video with the teacher's instructions for the activity. Carry out the activity with your group, following the teacher's instructions.

Observe and reflect on what **language functions** you need to use to carry out this activity. Please use the space below to jot down your observations/reflections:

2.4

Name of Activity or Lesson Explored: *How Many Raisins in a Box?, 4th Grade*

Focal Student Pseudonym: *Ariel*

Learning Areas (based on Barringer, Pohlman, & Robinson, 2010; Levine, 2002; Pohlman, 2008)	What are the demands of the lesson or activity? What roles do these learning areas play in the Raisin activity?	How does Ariel respond to the demands of the activity? Please note strengths and needs below.	How did Cristian Solorza change the activity, and what teaching practices does he use to make it more accessible to all students, including Ariel? What additional changes would you make?
Language • understands and uses mathematical language (e.g., math vocabulary, concrete and abstract language, contextualized and decontextualized language)			
• using language to communicate with others and to clarify ideas (e.g., understands spoken and written directions, uses spoken and written language to explain one's thinking)			
• using language to develop and master abstract concepts (e.g., verbalizes ideas to push one's thinking, uses language to connect an idea with a visual model)			
• demonstrates higher language function (e.g., understands and uses language that is technical, inferential, symbolic, and abstract)			

2.5

Higher Thinking • using and forming concepts • solving problems • logical thinking • creative and critical thinking				
Spatial Ordering • interpreting relationships within and between spatial patterns • organizing things in space • reasoning with images				
Sequential Ordering • organizing information in sequence • following directions • managing time				
Memory • short-term memory • active working memory • long-term memory				
Attention • controlling mental energy • maintaining focus • self-monitoring				
Psychosocial • social language • collaboration • conflict resolution				
Motor Coordination • gross motor functions • fine motor functions • grapho-motor functions				

WORKSHOP 2   **WORKSHEET 2C: LEARNING GOALS**

Your Name: _____ Focal Student Pseudonym: _____

Name of the Lesson: _____

Review the introductory pages of the unit guide for the *How Many Raisins in the Box?* lesson to help you answer the questions below. The unit overview is found on pages 56 (2.9) to 63 (2.16). The lesson is on pages 64 (2.17) to 74 (2.27).

1. What are the learning goals of the lesson?

2. In what ways do you think this lesson connects to what students have studied in math before (this school year and before)?

3. How do you think what students learn in this lesson will help them with the math they will learn in the future (this school year and beyond)?

| WORKSHOP 2 | WORKSHEET 2D: TEACHING PRACTICES THAT ENHANCE LEARNING FOR SECOND LANGUAGE LEARNERS AND STUDENTS WITH LANGUAGE PROCESSING PROBLEMS |

Second language learners and students with language processing problems can miss out on learning mathematics content and concepts. Researchers have found that teachers can promote learning of content subject matter by incorporating certain practices into their instruction. These are among the practices they recommend. Think about your focal child (or another child from your classroom). Which of the following teaching practices might work for him or her? How would you use these practices?

Teaching Practices	How would you use these practices with your focal student and other students in your classroom?
1. Language is simplified but content is robust.	
2. Demonstrate using materials.	
3. Have students use mathematical tools; hands-on learning.	
4. Make what you write readable by students. Pictures may be helpful.	
5. Make use of all senses.	
6. Bring the real world into the classroom.	
7. Adapt the materials to make them more accessible for the children you are teaching.	
8. Pair language minority students with native speakers.	
9. Give students responsibility for their own learning.	
10. Review instructions.	

2.8

Unit Guide for "How Many Raisins in a Box?" Lesson

UNIT OVERVIEW

The Shape of the Data

Content of This Unit   This unit provides students with some tools to record, represent, and analyze simple data sets about familiar situations. Students define issues and questions about data they collect. They organize data in rough draft and presentation graphs and look at the shape of the data—the patterns and special features—identifying places where there is a concentration of data (clumps) or where there are no data (holes). Students describe what seems to be typical for a set of data.

Connections with Other Units   If you are doing the full-year *Investigations* curriculum in the suggested sequence for grade 4, this is the sixth of eleven units. Most fourth graders will have the prerequisite measuring skills (as introduced in the third grade unit *From Paces to Feet*), but if they have had little experience with linear measurement, you may want to add an extra day or two at the beginning of Investigation 2 to give them extra practice measuring lengths, such as their height.

This unit can also be used as an introduction to statistics for fifth graders or even older students. The work in this unit is continued in the Data and Fractions unit, *Three out of Four Like Spaghetti*.

Investigations Curriculum ■ Suggested Grade 4 Sequence

Mathematical Thinking at Grade 4 (Introduction)

Arrays and Shares (Multiplication and Division)

Seeing Solids and Silhouettes (3-D Geometry)

Landmarks in the Thousands (The Number System)

Different Shapes, Equal Pieces (Fractions)

▶ *The Shape of the Data* (Statistics)

Money, Miles, and Large Numbers (Addition and Subtraction)

Changes Over Time (Graphs)

Packages and Groups (Multiplication and Division)

Sunken Ships and Grid Patterns (2-D Geometry)

Three out of Four Like Spaghetti (Data and Fractions)

Investigation 1 ■ Introduction to Data Analysis

Class Sessions	Activities	Pacing
Session 1 (p. 4) HOW MANY RAISINS IN A BOX?	Getting Acquainted with Statistics Estimating the Number of Raisins Collecting, Recording, and Organizing the Data Describing the Raisin Data Extension: Counting Other Groups Extension: Adding Data	minimum 1 hr
Sessions 2 and 3 (p. 13) HOW MANY PEOPLE IN A FAMILY?	How to Count Who's in Your Family What's the Shape of These Data? How Many Brothers and Sisters? Homework: How Many Brothers and Sisters? Extension: Adding More Family Data Extension: Census Data	minimum 2 hr

Ten-Minute Math ■ Estimation and Number Sense

Mathematical Emphasis	Assessment Resources	Materials
■ Making quick sketches of the data to use as working tools during the analysis process ■ Describing the shape of the data, moving from noticing individual features of the data to describing the overall shape of the distribution ■ Defining the way data will be collected ■ Summarizing what is typical of a set of data	Sketch Graphs: Quick to Make, Easy to Read (Teacher Note, p. 8) The Shape of the Data: Clumps, Bumps, and Holes (Teacher Note, p. 10) Describing the Shape of the Data (Dialogue Box, p. 12) Summarizing Data: What's Typical? (Teacher Note, p. 19)	Small boxes of raisins Unlined paper Concrete materials for representing data (optional) Overhead projector and transparencies Student Sheet 1 Family letter

Unit Overview ■ **I-13**

Investigation 2 ▪ Landmarks in the Data

Class Sessions	Activities	Pacing
Session 1 (p. 22) HOW TALL ARE FOURTH GRADERS?	Teacher Checkpoint: Line Plots and What's Typical Measuring Heights in This Class Describing the Class Height Data Comparing Our Class with Other Fourth Grades Homework: How Tall Are Fourth Graders?	minimum 1 hr
Sessions 2 and 3 (p. 28) FOURTH AND FIRST GRADERS: HOW MUCH TALLER?	Measuring First Graders' Heights Comparing Two Sets of Data Publishing Findings	minimum 2 hr
Session 4 (p. 33) LOOKING AT MYSTERY DATA	Describing Mystery Data A Teacher Checkpoint: Mystery Data B and C Homework: Looking at Mystery Data	minimum 1 hr
Session 5 (p. 39) FINDING THE MEDIAN	Finding the Median Height for This Class What's the Median Height of the All-Stars? Homework: How Many Cavities?	minimum 1 hr
Sessions 6 and 7 (p. 45) USING LANDMARKS IN DATA	Organizing Data and Finding the Median Another Mystery Data Set Assessment: Who Has More Cavities?	minimum 2 hr

◓ Ten-Minute Math ▪ Estimation and Number Sense, Broken Calculator

Mathematical Emphasis

- Inventing ways to compare and represent two sets of data by describing the shape of the data and what's typical of the data

- Finding the median in a set of data arranged in numerical order (e.g., when students line up in order by height)

- Finding the median in a set of data grouped by frequency (e.g., on a line plot or other graph)

- Using the median to describe a set of data and to compare one data set to another

Assessment Resources

Teacher Checkpoint: Line Plots and What's Typical (p. 23)

Measuring Heights: Using Tools (Teacher Note, p. 26)

Discussing Invented Methods for Finding Typical Values (Dialogue Box, p. 27)

How Can We Compare Our Class with a First Grade Class? (Dialogue Box, p. 32)

Teacher Checkpoint: Mystery Data B and C (p. 34)

Visualizing Measurement Data (Dialogue Box, p. 38)

What Good Is Knowing the Median? (Dialogue Box, p. 44)

Assessment: Who Has More Cavities? (p. 46)

Common Misconceptions About the Median . . . and How to Help (Dialogue Box, p. 47)

How Many Cavities Do We Have? (Dialogue Box, p. 48)

Materials

Chart paper (optional)

Unlined paper

Measuring tools

Calculators

Art materials for making presentation graphs

Overhead projector

Concrete materials for representing data (optional)

Student Sheets 2–11

Teaching resource sheets

I-14 ▪ *The Shape of the Data*

Investigation 3 ▪ A Data Project: Investigating Sleep

Class Sessions	Activities	Pacing
Sessions 1 and 2 (p. 52) WHAT DO WE WANT TO FIND OUT?	How Long Do People Sleep? Choosing a Question Working with Preliminary Data Homework: Three Nights' Sleep	minimum 2 hr
Sessions 3, 4, and 5 (p. 59) THE RESEARCH TEAM AT WORK	Collecting, Organizing, and Describing Data Developing Theories and Publishing Findings Assessment: Group Presentations Choosing Student Work to Save Homework: Wake Up! Homework: Representing How People Wake Up	minimum 3 hr

🕐 Ten-Minute Math ▪ Broken Calculator

Mathematical Emphasis	Assessment Resources	Materials
▪ Undertaking a complete data analysis project, from defining a question to publishing results ▪ Carrying out all the stages of a data analysis investigation ▪ Choosing and refining a research question ▪ Viewing the data in several different ways, using quick sketches and other representations to organize and display the data	I Wanna Do It Myself! (Teacher Note, p. 57) Helping Students Refine Their Questions (Dialogue Box, p. 58) Assessment: Group Presentations (p. 60) Choosing Student Work to Save (p. 61) Assessment: Group Presentations (Teacher Note, p. 62)	Materials for making initial representations of data Overhead projector Art materials for "publishing" results Student Sheets 12–14 Teaching resource sheets

MATERIALS LIST

Following are the basic materials needed for the activities in this unit.

- Small (half-ounce) boxes of raisins: at least 1 per student. (Or, use small packages of other easily countable things that are packed by weight, such as peanuts.)
- Snap™ Cubes (interlocking cubes), counting chips, or other concrete material for representing the data: about 150–200 (optional)
- Measuring tools—yardsticks, metersticks, or tape measures—1 per group of students
- Chart paper for recording data (optional)
- Unlined paper for making sketch graphs
- Materials for making presentation graphs—a variety of paper including one-inch or one-centimeter graph paper, colored markers or crayons, scissors, glue
- Calculators
- Overhead projector

The following materials are provided at the end of this unit as blackline masters. A Student Activity Booklet containing all student sheets and teaching resources needed for individual work is available.

Family Letter (p. 72)

Student Sheets 1–14 (p. 73)

Teaching Resources:

    '93 All-Star Cards (p. 84)

    Sleep Table (p. 90)

    One-Centimeter Graph Paper (p. 91)

Practice Pages (p. 93)

Related Children's Literature

Anno, Mitsumasa. *Anno's Magic Seeds.* New York: Philomel Books, 1995.

Rylant, Cynthia. *The Relatives Came.* New York: Bradbury Press, 1985.

Winthrop, Elizabeth. *Shoes.* New York: Harper and Row, 1986.

A Note on Measuring Tools   For measuring student heights in Investigation 2, Session 1, you may decide to use either metric or U.S. Standard units. Tape measures calibrated in either centimeters or inches are very useful here.

Some schools may have a combination measuring tool—metersticks that are 100 centimeters long, but that are also calibrated in inches on the reverse. These are fine for use with metric measure; however, be careful if you plan to use them for measuring in inches. They look like yardsticks, but they are actually a little more than 39 inches long. This can be confusing to students (and adults) who use this tool, expecting to measure things in 3-foot lengths.

To reduce the confusion, try covering the extra 3 inches with masking tape when students need yardsticks. When you distribute these tools, explain why you have covered the end. If you can get separate yardsticks and metersticks, use these instead of the combination stick.

ABOUT THE MATHEMATICS IN THIS UNIT

People construct much of their knowledge of the world through informal analysis of data they encounter. When we decide that 10:00 P.M. is too late to call a friend, we are basing our actions on data we have noted in the course of our daily lives—that is, most of our friends go to bed around 10, and don't like to be bothered just as they are going to bed. When we decide to make two dozen brownies for a party for six people, it's because we've seen people eat as many as four brownies at a time. Every day, we collect and analyze data in informal ways. Children are no exception. They notice patterns in such data as people's heights, the sizes of pets, and the number of students present in class each day.

The ability to analyze data critically is becoming a prerequisite of democratic life and productive work in the late twentieth century. Unfortunately, these skills have been almost completely absent from schools until the last decade or so. In that time, we have learned that elementary school students can easily work with basic statistical ideas and that they are enthusiastic about collecting and understanding data. The mathematics of data connect to their natural curiosity about the world around them.

This unit presents just a few critical concepts about data, yet those concepts are the basis of practically all statistical thinking. Being able to describe and compare the patterns and special features of data—the shape of the data—is what statistics is really all about. Looking at the way data are distributed provides the basis for interpreting the data as a whole. This unit gives students an introduction to the following processes:

- asking good statistical questions
- recording and organizing collected data
- drawing quick graphs to get a sense of the data
- drawing more precise graphs to look at details of the data
- finding landmarks in the data, including the median
- considering how to describe the "typical" person/measurement in a data set

Working with data provides opportunities for students to use a variety of mathematical skills. For example, talking about the range of a data set and the existence of outliers is related to an understanding of the base ten system. Figuring out the median of a data set involves some counting and division (There are 37 data points; which is the middle one?) as well as more abstract thinking to consider what the median actually says about a data set. The computation students do in data analysis is purposeful, and the analysis they do helps them to understand how mathematics can function as a significant tool for describing, comparing, predicting, and making decisions.

Mathematical Emphasis At the beginning of each investigation, the Mathematical Emphasis section tells you what is most important for students to learn about during that investigation. Many of these mathematical understandings and processes are difficult and complex. Students gradually learn more and more about each idea over many years of schooling. Individual students will begin and end the unit with different levels of knowledge and skill, but all will gain greater knowledge about how we collect, represent, describe, and interpret data from the real world.

2.14

ABOUT THE ASSESSMENT IN THIS UNIT

Throughout the *Investigations* curriculum, there are many opportunities for ongoing daily assessment as you observe, listen to, and interact with students at work. In this unit, you will find two Teacher Checkpoints:

Investigation 2, Session 1:
Line Plots and What's Typical (p. 23)

Investigation 2, Session 4:
Mystery Data B and C (p. 34)

This unit also has two embedded Assessment activities:

Investigation 2, Sessions 6–7:
Who Has More Cavities? (p. 46)

Investigation 3, Sessions 3–5:
Group Presentations (p. 60)

In addition, you can use almost any activity in this unit to assess your students' needs and strengths. Listed below are questions to help you focus your observations in each investigation. You may want to keep track of your observations for each student to help you plan your curriculum and monitor students' growth. Suggestions for documenting student growth can be found in the section About Assessment (p. I-10).

Investigation 1: Introduction to Data Analysis

- What kinds of quick sketches of the data do students make to use as working tools during the analysis process? Do these give a clear picture of the shape of the data?
- How do students describe the shape of the data? Do they notice patterns and trends in the data, or do they look only at individual numbers in a data set? How do they describe where most of the data are, where there are no data, and where there are isolated pieces of data?
- What approaches do students use to summarize data? Do their ways of determining what is "typical" reflect a growing understanding of the center of the data?

Investigation 2: Landmarks in the Data

- What ways do students come up with to compare and represent two sets of data? Do they describe the shape of the data and what's typical of the data?

- What inventive and creative ways have students found to construct their presentation graphs? Do these presentations give an organized, clear, and accessible display of the data? Do they support what students have found in their analyses by directing attention to important features of the data?
- Are students able to find the median in a set of data arranged in numerical order (e.g., when students line up in order by height)?
- Are students able to find the median in a set of data grouped by frequency (e.g., on a line plot or other graph)?
- Are students able to use the median and other landmarks in the data to describe a set of data and to compare one data set to another?

Investigation 3: A Data Project: Investigating Sleep

- How do students go about planning and completing a full data analysis investigation, from deciding the question to creating the final report?
- How do students choose and refine a research question?
- How do students collect and display data?
- How valid are students' conclusions? How comprehensive is their report? Are they able to critique their own investigation (e.g., relationship to other ideas in the unit, limitations of the study, aspects of the research that they might do differently next time, questions they might ask)?
- Are students able to make sense of different representations for organizing and displaying data?

Assessment Sourcebook

In the *Assessment Sourcebook* you will find End-of-Unit Assessment Tasks and Assessment Masters available in English and Spanish. You will also find suggestions to help you observe and evaluate student work and checklists of mathematical emphases with space for you to record individual student information.

PREVIEW FOR THE LINGUISTICALLY DIVERSE CLASSROOM

In the *Investigations* curriculum, mathematical vocabulary is introduced naturally during the activities. We don't ask students to learn definitions of new terms; rather, they come to understand such words as *factor* or *area* or *symmetry* by hearing them used frequently in discussion as they investigate new concepts. This approach is compatible with current theories of second-language acquisition, which emphasize the use of new vocabulary in meaningful contexts while students are actively involved with objects, pictures, and physical movement.

Listed below are some key words used in this unit that will not be new to most English speakers at this age level, but may be unfamiliar to students with limited English proficiency. You will want to spend additional time working on these words with your students who are learning English. If your students are working with a second-language teacher, you might enlist your colleague's aid in familiarizing students with these words, before and during this unit. In the classroom, look for opportunities for students to hear and use these words. Activities you can use to present the words are given in the appendix, Vocabulary Support for Second-Language Learners (p. 69).

height, tall Students measure their own and younger children's *heights*, comparing the results and determining how *tall* typical fourth graders and first graders are; they also use height data in other activities.

pounds, weigh Students will use these terms in analyzing data that report the weights of domestic cats and lions in zoos.

family, people, children (kids) Students collect data on the size of families, and must first decide which people to count as part of "a family."

sleep, time These terms are a key part of the culminating project—an open-ended investigation involving how much time people spend sleeping each day, based on their bedtimes and wake-up times.

In addition to these key words, students will encounter terms related to dental work *(cavities, teeth, dentist)*. Familiarity with these words will be helpful as they work on the assessment activity in Investigation 2, Who Has More Cavities?

Multicultural Extensions for All Students

Whenever possible, encourage students to share words, objects, customs, or any aspects of daily life from their cultures and backgrounds that are relevant to the activities in this unit. For example:

- In Investigation 1, when counting raisins in small snack-size boxes, let students suggest other snack items familiar to them, sold in small packages, that could be similarly counted.

- When the students are discussing family size later in Investigation 1, they might bring in family photos to post. Ask for the words that define the members of a family in the cultures represented in your classroom. Encourage the class to compare and learn the words in different languages for *mother, father, brother, sister*.

2.16

INVESTIGATION 1

Introduction to Data Analysis

What Happens

Session 1: How Many Raisins in a Box?
Students count the raisins in a sample of small
boxes of raisins (one box for each student), record
and organize the results, and describe the shape
of the data distribution. The line plot is introduced as a useful way to make a first-draft visual
representation of a set of data.

**Sessions 2 and 3: How Many People in a
Family?** Students decide how to determine family size for their class, then collect family size
data in their classroom. They describe the shape
of the distribution of family size for their class
and determine typical family size from these data.
They compare it with the typical family size in
their community.

Mathematical Emphasis

■ Making quick sketches of the data to use as
working tools during the analysis process

■ Describing the shape of the data, moving from
noticing individual features of the data ("Two
boxes had 33 raisins, three boxes had 34
raisins") to describing the overall shape of
the distribution ("Over half of the boxes had
between 34 and 37 raisins")

■ Defining the way data will be collected

■ Summarizing what is typical of a set of data

2 ■ Investigation 1: Introduction to Data Analysis

INVESTIGATION 1

What to Plan Ahead of Time

Materials

- Small (half-ounce) boxes of raisins, at least 1 per student. Alternative: Small packages of other easily countable things that are packed by weight, such as peanuts (Session 1)
- Unlined paper for making sketch graphs (Sessions 1–3)
- Interlocking cubes or a similar concrete material for representing the data, about 750 (Sessions 2–3, optional)
- Overhead projector (Sessions 2–3)
- Blank overhead transparencies and pen (Sessions 2–3)

Other Preparation

- Become familiar with making a line plot. See the **Teacher Note,** Sketch Graphs: Quick to Make, Easy to Read (p. 8) and the **Teacher Note,** Line Plots: A Quick Way to Show the Shape of the Data (p. 9).
- Plan to save the empty raisin boxes (Session 1) and the family data (Sessions 2–3) to use in Investigation 2, Session 5.
- Find out the typical family size for your community. Municipal government offices are usually glad to provide this information over the phone. Typically, the figure will be the mean family size in decimal form (e.g., 3.24). The use of decimals is not recommended for this investigation; "about 3" or "between 3 and 4" is accurate enough. (Sessions 2–3)
- Prepare copies of your class list, 1 per student, for recording data. (Sessions 2–3, optional)
- Duplicate student sheets and teaching resources (located at the end of this unit) as follows. If you have Student Activity Booklets, copy only the item marked with an asterisk.

  For Sessions 2–3

  Student Sheet 1, How Many Brothers and Sisters? (p. 73): 1 per student (homework)

  Family letter* (p. 72): 1 per student. Remember to sign it before copying.

- If you plan to provide folders in which students will save their work for the entire unit, prepare these for distribution during Session 1.

Investigation 1: Introduction to Data Analysis ■ **3**

Session 1

How Many Raisins in a Box?

Materials

- Half-ounce boxes of raisins (1 per student)
- Unlined paper

What Happens

Students count the raisins in a sample of small boxes of raisins (one box for each student), record and organize the results, and describe the shape of the data distribution. The line plot is introduced as a useful way to make a first-draft visual representation of a set of data. Student work focuses on:

- recording the collected data
- organizing the data
- sketching a graph of the data
- examining the shape of the data

Activity

Getting Acquainted with Statistics

This year, as part of our mathematics work, we will be studying statistics. Have you ever heard the word *statistics*? Can you give me any examples of statistics?

Students may know about the use of statistics in sports or in opinion polls.

Statistics is the study of data. Data give us information about something in the real world. We can collect some data right now. How many people in this room have a pet (have brown eyes, speak Spanish, once lived in a different country, take the bus to school)?

Ask several of these questions, count the student responses, and point out that these are data (for example, "Our data show that 12 students in this class take the bus to school").

People collect data by counting, as we just did, or by measuring or by doing experiments. Who can think of some data we can collect by measuring?

Students may think of examples such as the size of the classroom, their heights, or the distance from home to school. Encourage them to think of measures involving weight, volume, time, or temperature, as well.

After mathematicians or scientists have collected their data, they study the data carefully and look for patterns that could tell them something important. For example, data about traffic accidents might give information about which kinds of cars are the safest or whether seat belts make a difference. Data about the number of fish in certain lakes or rivers could give clues about the effects of water pollution.

If possible, provide an example of the use of statistics in your school or community. For example, in one school, a particular piece of playground equipment was forbidden to students younger than fourth grade. The principal used data about injuries on this piece of equipment to make a decision about who could use it. Many of the younger students, it turned out, did not have big enough hands to grasp the bars securely.

Just like mathematicians and scientists who use statistics, we can collect data to find out information about ourselves or the world around us. Today, we are going to start by collecting data about something familiar—a box of raisins.

Activity

Estimating the Number of Raisins

Give a box of raisins to each student. Ask students to keep the boxes closed.

Does anybody have an idea about how many raisins there are in a box this size?

Let students offer their ideas. Some may think that because the boxes have the same weight, they have the same number of raisins. Some may think that it would be too hard to put the same number in each box. Have students open their boxes so they can see the top layer of raisins.

What do you think now? Do you want to revise your estimate?

Allow enough time for students to discuss all their ideas. Then pose follow-up questions, for example:

Why do you think there will be about 50? Your idea is very different from Luisa's; how did each of you arrive at your estimate? Will the number of raisins in each box be the same or different? Why do you think so?

Session 1: How Many Raisins in a Box? ▪ **5**

Activity

Collecting, Recording, and Organizing the Data

Students open their boxes and count the raisins. As they finish their counts, they report their data. Record the numbers in a list on the chalkboard, in whatever order they are reported.

If we wanted to organize these data better, what could we do?

Take a few suggestions from the students. Then have them work in pairs or groups of three, each group choosing one way to organize the data quickly and making a sketch to show it. Emphasize that this is a rough draft sketch; it need not be done meticulously. Once students have organized the data, each group should write down three important things they can say about their data.

Ask a few students to demonstrate their methods for organizing the data, or quickly demonstrate them yourself on the board. Make sure that all the types of representation students have invented are demonstrated. See the **Teacher Note**, Sketch Graphs: Quick to Make, Easy to Read (p. 8).

Mathematicians have invented ways of showing data, too. Here's one way that's easy to use. It's called a *line plot*.

Organize the raisin data on a line plot large enough for everyone to see. For explanation and an example, see the **Teacher Note**, Line Plots: A Quick Way to Show the Shape of the Data (p. 9).

Activity

Describing the Raisin Data

What are some of the things you wrote down about these data?

Help students express their initial ideas. To help them get started on this complex question, see the **Teacher Note**, The Shape of the Data: Clumps, Bumps, and Holes (p. 10). The **Teacher Note**, Range and Outliers (p. 11), talks about terms useful in discussing data.

❖ **Tip for the Linguistically Diverse Classroom** Encourage students with limited English proficiency to come up and point to the line plot, using gestures and single words to communicate what they notice about the shape of the data, as you help them verbalize their ideas.

What else can you say about these data? Does anyone have another way to describe this representation? Suppose someone asked you, "About how many raisins are in a box?" What could you say?

6 ■ *Investigation 1: Introduction to Data Analysis*

See the **Dialogue Box,** Describing the Shape of the Data (p. 12), for a sample discussion.

Making Predictions Ask students to speculate about what adding new information would do to the shape of the data.

If we opened five more boxes of raisins, what is your best guess about how many raisins would be in them, based on the data we already have?

Students work on this question for a few minutes in small groups, then report their theories back to the whole class. Expect them to give reasons for their ideas. Encourage students to ask each other questions and to discuss reasons for the differences among their ideas.

At the end of the session, have each student write inside the top flap the number of raisins found in that box. Then allow students to eat the raisins. Collect and save the boxes for use as a data set in Investigation 2 of this unit.

Session 1 Follow-Up

Counting Other Groups Try a similar activity with other materials—packages of peanuts, packages of sunflower seeds, or fresh peas in pods. What is the shape of the data this time? Is it harder or easier to predict how many will be in a new package?

 **Extensions**

Adding Data Students are very interested in what happens when they add to their data. Have students count the raisins in extra boxes and add their findings to the class data. Or, keep the class data posted and add to them periodically. Do these additional data change the shape of the data distribution in any way? You could use the raisin boxes themselves to make a more permanent display.

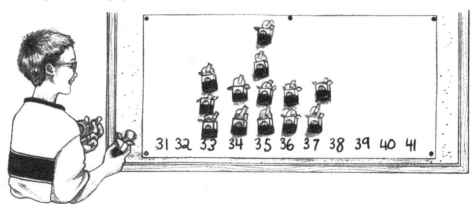

Session 1: How Many Raisins in a Box? ▪ **7**

2.22

Teacher Note

Sketch Graphs: Quick to Make, Easy to Read

Graphing is often taught as an art of presentation, the end point of the data analysis process, the means for communicating what has been found. Certainly, a pictorial representation is an effective way to present data to an audience at the end of an investigation. But graphs, tables, diagrams, and charts are also data analysis tools. A user of statistics employs pictures and graphs frequently during the process of analysis in order to better understand the data.

Many working graphs need never be shown to anyone else. Students can make and use them just to help uncover the story of the data. We call such representations *sketch graphs* or *rough draft graphs*.

We want students to become comfortable with a variety of such working graphs. Sketch graphs should be easy to make and easy to read; they should not challenge students' patience or fine motor skills. Unlike graphs for presentation, sketch graphs do not require neatness, careful measurement or scaling, use of clear titles or labels, or decorative work.

Sketch graphs:

- can be made rapidly
- reveal aspects of the shape of the data
- are clear, but not necessarily neat
- don't require labels or titles (as long as students are clear about what the graphs represent)
- don't require time-consuming attention to color or design

Encourage students to invent different forms of sketch graphs until they discover some that work well in organizing their data. Sketch graphs may be made with pencil and paper, with interlocking cubes, or with stick-on notes. Cubes and stick-on notes in particular offer flexibility because they can easily be rearranged.

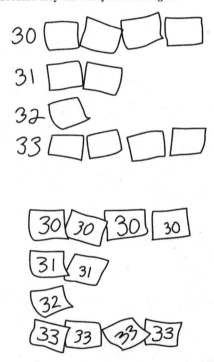

30 ✓ ✓ ✓ ✓
31 ✓ ✓
32 ✓
33 ✓ ✓ ✓ ✓

```
X                    X
X                    X
x        X           X
X        x      X    X
30      31      32   33
```

Line Plots: A Quick Way to Show the Shape of the Data

> **Teacher Note**

A line plot is a quick way to organize numerical data. It clearly shows the range of the data, the interval from the lowest to the highest value, and how the data are distributed over that range. Line plots work especially well for numerical data with a small range, such as the number of raisins in a box.

A line plot is most often used as a working graph and is especially useful as an initial organizing tool for work with a data set. It need not include a title, labels, or a vertical axis. A line plot is simply a sketch showing the values of the data along a horizontal axis and X's to mark the frequency of those values. For example, a line plot showing the number of raisins in 15 boxes might be drawn as shown below.

From this display, we can quickly see that two-thirds of the boxes have either 37 or 38 raisins.

Although the range is from 30 to 38, the interval in which most data fall is from 35 to 38. The outlier, at 30, appears to be an unusual value, separated by a considerable gap from the rest of the data.

One advantage of a line plot is that each piece of data can be recorded directly on the graph as it is collected. To set up a line plot, students start with an initial guess about what the range of the data is likely to be: What should we put as the lowest number? How high should we go? Leave some room on each end so that you can lengthen the line later if the range includes lower or higher values than you expected.

By quickly sketching data in line plots on the chalkboard, you provide a model of using such graphs to get a quick, clear picture of the shape of the data.

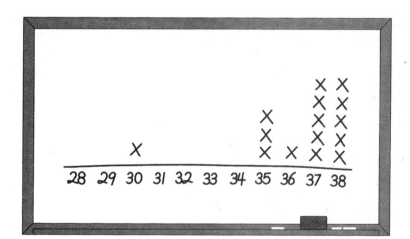

Session 1: How Many Raisins in a Box? ▪ **9**

2.24

> ### Teacher Note

The Shape of the Data: Clumps, Bumps, and Holes

Describing and interpreting data is a skill that must be acquired. Too often, students simply read numbers or other information from a graph or table without any interpretation or understanding. It is easy for students to notice only isolated bits of information ("Vanilla got the most votes" or "Five people were 50 inches tall") without developing an overall sense of what the graph shows. To help students pay attention to the shape of the data—the patterns and special features—we have found useful such words as *clumps, clusters, bumps, gaps, holes, spread out,* and *bunched together.* Encourage students to use this casual language to describe where most of the data are, where there are no data, and where there are isolated pieces of data.

A discussion of the shape of the data often breaks down into two stages. First, we decide what are the special features of the shape: Where are the clumps or clusters, the gaps, the outliers? Are the data spread out, or are lots of the data clustered around a few values? Second, we decide how we can interpret the shape of these data: Do we have theories or experiences that might account for how the data are distributed?

As an example, consider the graph at right, which shows the weight in pounds of 23 lions in U.S. zoos. (Note that this example is for teacher use only; the same data will be presented as Mystery Data in Investigation 2, Landmarks in the Data.) In the first stage of discussion, one group of students observed the following special features:

■ There is a clump of lions between 400 and 475 pounds (about a third).

■ There is another cluster centering around 300 pounds (another third).

■ There are two pairs of much lighter lions, separated by a gap from the rest of the data.

In the second stage of discussion, students considered what might account for the shape of these data. They immediately theorized that the four lightest lions must be cubs. They were, in fact, one litter of 4-month-old cubs in the Miami Zoo. The other two clusters turned out to reflect the difference between the weights of adult male and female lions.

Throughout this unit, we strive to steer students away from merely reading or calculating numbers drawn from their data (the range was 23 to 48, the median was 90, the biggest height was 52 inches). These numbers are useful only when they are seen in the context of the overall shape and patterns of the data and when they lead to questioning and theory building. By focusing instead on the broader picture—the shape of the data—we discover what the data can tell us about the world.

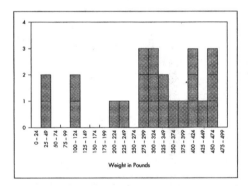

Weight in Pounds

2.25

Range and Outliers

<blockquote>Teacher Note</blockquote>

Range and *outlier* are two statistical ideas that come up naturally in discussing data with students.

The range of the data is simply the interval from the lowest value to the highest value in the data set. The range of the data in the line plot below, which shows how many raisins were in each of 15 boxes of raisins, is from 30 to 38.

An *outlier* is an individual piece of data that has an unusual value, much lower or much higher than most of the data. It "lies outside" the overall shape and pattern of the data. There is no one definition of how far away from the rest of the data a value must be to be termed an outlier. Although statisticians have rules of thumb for finding outliers, these are always subject to judgment about a particular data set. As you view the shape of the data, you and your stu-

dents must judge whether there are values that don't seem to fit with the rest of the data. For example, in the raisin data, the box containing 30 raisins seems to be an outlier. A family of 12 is likely to be an outlier in family size data.

Both range and outliers are ideas that will come up naturally in this unit. They can be introduced as soon as they arise in the students' descriptions of their data. Students easily learn the correct terms for these ideas and are particularly interested in outliers.

Outliers should be examined closely. Sometimes they turn out to be mistakes—someone counted, measured, or recorded incorrectly—but other times they are simply unusual values. Students are generally very interested in building theories about these odd values: What might account for them?

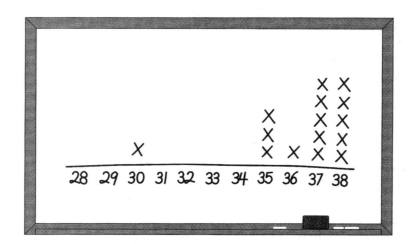

Describing the Shape of the Data

This discussion took place during the activity Describing the Raisin Data (p. 6). Students are looking at their line plot.

```
              x
          x   x  x
      x   x   x  x   x
      x   x   x  x   x      x              x
     ─────────────────────────────────────────
      31 32 33 34 35 36 37 38 39 40 41 42 43
```

So what can you say about the raisin data? Let's hear a few of your ideas.

Kim: Well, there are a lot at 35.

Alex: There was only one at 39 and one at 43.

Rikki: There are two at 33 and 34.

Karen: And 33 is the lowest.

So no boxes had fewer than 33 raisins?

David: Yeah. And 43 was the highest.

So the range was from 33 to 43. What else?

Jesse: There's nothing at 38, 40, 41, or 42.

Jesse's noticing that there are a lot of holes in this part of the data. Can anyone say any more about that?

Lina Li: Well, there's nothing at 31 or 32 either.

Yes, 33 is the lowest count and there's nothing below it. But the situation that Jesse noticed up here is a little different. What can you say about that?

Kumiko: Mostly, the raisins go from 33 to 37, but sometimes you get something higher.

Can anyone add to that?

B.J.: You'd be really lucky if you were the one who got 43!

Mathematicians have a name for a piece of data that is far away from all the rest. They call it an *outlier*. An outlier is an unusual piece of data—sometimes it's an error, but sometimes it's just an unusual piece of data. It's often interesting to try to find out more about an outlier. Who had this outlier?

Emilio: I did. And I counted twice, and Kyle checked it, too, so I know it was 43.

Rikki: Maybe he's got smaller raisins.

Any other theories about Emilio's box?

Lesley Ann: Maybe it doesn't really weigh the same as the other boxes. Maybe too many raisins got dropped in when it was going through the factory.

… [*Later*] So if someone asked you, "What's the typical number of raisins in a box?"—what would you say?

Irena: Well, I'd say 35.

[*Addressing the class as a whole*] **Why would 35 be a reasonable description of how many raisins are in a box?**

DeShane: Because the most boxes had 35.

Any other ways to say this? Or any different ideas?

Kyle: Well, I wouldn't say just 35.

Why not?

Kyle: Well, there's really not that much difference between 33, 34, 35, 36. They're all really close together. I'd say 33 to 37, 'cause the 39 and 43 aren't what you'd usually get.

So Kyle is saying he'd use an interval to describe the raisins, from 33 to 37, and Irena said she'd say 35 was typical. What do other people think about that?

In this discussion, the class has moved gradually from describing individual features of the data to looking at the shape of the data as a whole. The teacher introduced the terms *interval*, *range*, and *outlier* as they came up naturally in the discussion. Throughout, the teacher asked students to give reasons for their ideas and pushed them to think further by asking for additions or alternatives to ideas students raised.

12 ▪ *Investigation 1: Introduction to Data Analysis*

Name **Ariel**   Date **April 1, 2004**

INSTRUCTIONS: Count your *raisins*. Then **ask your partner** the **questions** below.

> REMEMBER! DO NOT EAT THE RAISINS!..(At least, not until later!)

QUESTIONS
Answer these YES or NO questions.   ⟨ CIRCLE ONE ⟩

1. Did you count your raisins by 1s?   Y   N
2. Did you count your raisins in multiples of 5s?   Y   N
3. Did you count your raisins in multiples of 10s?   Y   N
4. If you did NOT count in multiples of 1s, 5s, or 10s, *how* did you count?
   EXPLAIN your partners strategy in the space below.

5. How many *raisins* were in your box? __110__ *raisins*
   a. Please use one of the markers at your table to **WRITE** *your partner's*
      number on a Post-It.
   b. Write in **BIG NUMBERS** so we can see your number from far away.
   c. Place the Post-It on the board.

If you have time

At the rug, we collected data about how many people had dogs, brown eyes, and blue
jeans? We also found out how many people take the bus to school.

What other data can you collect? What information would you like to find out about your
class? *Make a list of questions in the table below.* (I started the table out for you.)

Data I can find out by counting	1. How many people in the class like *chocolate* ice cream? 2.
~~✗~~ 5	
Data I can find out by measuring 110	
Data I can find out by conducting experiments	

Name of group members: _Felix   Ariel_

Date _4/1/09_

OUR CLASS DATA:

How many raisins are in the box?

INSTRUCTIONS: Find a way to *organize the data* we collected. Use the data from the class Post-its. Make a rough draft sketch. (You will only have 10 minutes to do this.)

6 70
2 98
3 98
4 98
5 101
6 102
7 102
8
9
10
11
12
13 106

14 107
15 108
16 108
17 110
18 113
19 113
20 115
21 118
22 ← 22 ← W

What do you notice about your data? Write down three important things you can say about the data.

1. All the numbers are in order.

2. My number is the highest.

3. The last number is 70.

2.29

Name _Elix_   Date _4/1/04_

INSTRUCTIONS: Count your *raisins*. Then **ask your partner** the **questions** below.

REMEMBER! <u>DO NOT</u> EAT THE RAISINS!..(At least, not until later!)

QUESTIONS
Answer these YES or NO questions.   CIRCLE ONE

1. Did you count your raisins by 1s?   Y   N
2. Did you count your raisins in multiples of 5s?   Y   N
3. Did you count your raisins in multiples of 10s?   Y   N
4. If you did NOT count in multiples of 1s, 5s, or 10s, *how* did you count?
   EXPLAIN your partners strategy in the space below.

5. How many *raisins* were in your box? ⊪ 16 *raisins*
   a. **Please use one of the markers at your table to WRITE** *your partner's number* **on a Post-It.**
   b. **Write in BIG NUMBERS so we can see your number from far away.**
   c. **Place the Post-It on the board.**

· ·

If you have time

At the rug, we collected data about how many people had dogs, brown eyes, and blue jeans? We also found out how many people take the bus to school.

What other data can you collect? What information would you like to find out about your class? *Make a list of questions in the table below.* (I started the table out for you.)

Data I can find out by counting	1. How many people in the class like *chocolate* ice cream? 2.
Data I can find out by measuring	① how long is your table. ② how tall are you.
Data I can find out by conducting experiments	

Name of group members: Ariel   ²Filix   Date April 4 2004

OUR CLASS DATA:

How many raisins are in the box?

INSTRUCTIONS: Find a way to *organize the data* we collected. Use the data from the class Post-Its. Make a rough draft sketch. (You will only have 10 minutes to do this.)

① 70   ⑨ 102   ⑰ 10%   ㉔ 101
② 98   ⑩ 103   ⑱ 113,
③ 98   ⑪ 104
④ 98   ⑫ 105   ⑳ 113
⑤ 101   ⑬ 106   ㉒ 116
⑥ 101   ⑭ 107   ㉑ 118
⑦ 102   ⑮ 108   ㉓ 127
⑧ 102   ⑯ 108   ㉓ 115

What do you notice about your data? Write down three important things you can say about the data.

1. That I put them by low and then high.

2. That I puted all the numbers their.

3. That I cout all the numbers on the chart.

Name _Asher_   Date _5/1/01_

INSTRUCTIONS: Count your *raisins*. Then **ask your partner** the **questions** below.

> REMEMBER! DO NOT EAT THE RAISINS!..(At least, not until later!)

QUESTIONS
Answer these YES or NO questions. (CIRCLE ONE)

1. Did you count your raisins by 1s? (Y) N
2. Did you count your raisins in multiples of 5s? Y (N)
3. Did you count your raisins in multiples of 10s? Y (N)
4. If you did NOT count in multiples of 1s, 5s, or 10s, *how* did you count?
   EXPLAIN your partners strategy in the space below.

5. How many *raisins* were in your box? _101_ raisins
   a. Please use one of the markers at your table to WRITE *your partner's number* on a Post-It.
   b. Write in BIG NUMBERS so we can see your number from far away.
   c. Place the Post-It on the board.

- -

If you have time

At the rug, we collected data about how many people had dogs, brown eyes, and blue jeans? We also found out how many people take the bus to school.

What other data can you collect? What information would you like to find out about your class? *Make a list of questions in the table below.* (I started the table out for you.)

Data I can find out by counting	1. How many people in the class like *chocolate* ice cream? 2. How many people like basketball.
Data I can find out by measuring	
Data I can find out by conducting experiments	

Name _Jeffrey_ Date _4-1-04_

INSTRUCTIONS: Count your *raisins*. Then **ask your partner** the **questions** below.

REMEMBER! __DO NOT__ EAT THE RAISINS!..(At least, not until later!)

QUESTIONS
Answer these YES or NO questions. (CIRCLE ONE)

1. Did you count your raisins by 1s?   Y   (N)
2. Did you count your raisins in multiples of 5s?   Y   (N)
3. Did you count your raisins in multiples of 10s?   (Y)   N
4. If you did NOT count in multiples of 1s, 5s, or 10s, *how* did you count?
   EXPLAIN your partners strategy in the space below.

5. How many *raisins* were in your box? _98_ *raisins*
   a. Please use one of the markers at your table to WRITE *your partner's number* on a Post-It.
   b. Write in BIG NUMBERS so we can see your number from far away.
   c. Place the Post-It on the board.

. . . .

If you have time

At the rug, we collected data about how many people had dogs, brown eyes, and blue jeans? We also found out how many people take the bus to school.

What other data can you collect? What information would you like to find out about your class? *Make a list of questions in the table below.* (I started the table out for you.)

Data I can find out by counting	1. How many people in the class like *chocolate* ice cream? 2.
Data I can find out by measuring	
Data I can find out by conducting experiments	

2.33

Name of group members: Asher & Jeffrey

Date 4-1-09

OUR CLASS DATA:

How many raisins are in the box?

INSTRUCTIONS: Find a way to *organize the data* we collected. Use the data from the class Post-Its. Make a rough draft sketch. You will only have 10 minutes to do this.

101 102 103
103 101 101
103 101 101

102 105 106 110 115 98 109 106 106 116 108 108 113 113 79 107 107 102 110
                          98   108
                          99   108
                                            101

What do you notice about your data? Write down three important things you can say about the data.

1. Most of the numbers are 3 digits.

2. There all in the 100's

3. There are 26 people.

Name __Bappy__   Date __4/1/04__

INSTRUCTIONS: Count your *raisins*. Then **ask your partner the questions** below.

> REMEMBER! <u>DO NOT</u> EAT THE RAISINS!..(At least, not until later!)

QUESTIONS

Answer these YES or NO questions.   (CIRCLE ONE)

1. Did you count your raisins by 1s?   (Y)   N
2. Did you count your raisins in multiples of 5s?   Y   (N)
3. Did you count your raisins in multiples of 10s?   Y   (N)
4. If you did NOT count in multiples of 1s, 5s, or 10s, *how* did you count? EXPLAIN your partners strategy in the space below.

5. How many *raisins* were in your box? __102__ *raisins*
   a. Please use one of the markers at your table to WRITE *your partner's number* on a Post-It.
   b. Write in BIG NUMBERS so we can see your number from far away.
   c. Place the Post-It on the board.

. . . .

If you have time

At the rug, we collected data about how many people had dogs, brown eyes, and blue jeans? We also found out how many people take the bus to school.

What other data can you collect? What information would you like to find out about your class? ***Make a list of questions in the table below.*** (I started the table out for you.)

Data I can find out by counting	1. How many people in the class like *chocolate* ice cream? 2. How many people likes vanilla ice cream?
Data I can find out by measuring	1. How tall is your foot? 2. How tall are you?
Data I can find out by conducting experiments	1. How do magnets attract? 2. How do they repel?

Name _Aila_   Date _4/1/04_

INSTRUCTIONS: Count your *raisins*. Then **ask your partner** the questions below.

> REMEMBER! <u>DO NOT</u> EAT THE RAISINS!..(At least, not until later!)

QUESTIONS
Answer these YES or NO questions.   (CIRCLE ONE)

1. Did you count your raisins by 1s?   (Y)   N
2. Did you count your raisins in multiples of 5s?   Y   (N)
3. Did you count your raisins in multiples of 10s?   (Y)   N
4. If you did NOT count in multiples of 1s, 5s, or 10s, *how* did you count?
   EXPLAIN your partners strategy in the space below.

5. How many *raisins* were in your box? _106_ raisins
   a. Please use one of the markers at your table to WRITE *your partner's number* on a Post-It.
   b. Write in BIG NUMBERS so we can see your number from far away.
   c. Place the Post-It on the board.

• •

If you have time

At the rug, we collected data about how many people had dogs, brown eyes, and blue jeans? We also found out how many people take the bus to school.

What other data can you collect? What information would you like to find out about your class? ***Make a list of questions in the table below.*** (I started the table out for you.)

Data I can find out by counting	1. How many people in the class like *chocolate* ice cream? 2. How many people in the class likes music? 3. How many people in the class like dance with Roy?
Data I can find out by measuring	1. measuring my foot 2. measuring my pants. 3. measuring my hand.
Data I can find out by conducting experiments	

2.36

Name of group members: __Boppy & Alla__   Date __4/1/09__

OUR CLASS DATA:
How many raisins are in the box?

INSTRUCTIONS: Find a way to *organize the data* we collected. Use the data from the class Post-Its. Make a rough draft sketch. (You will only have 10 minutes to do this.)

Key
X = 1
person

4		4		3													4		

X X X X | X | X X X X | X | X | X | X | X | X | X | X | X | X | X | X X X X | X | X

102 | 105 | 107 | 101 | 110 | 115 | 101 | 9 8 | 104 | 106 | 118 | 116 | 109 | 108 | 114 | 113 | 103

What do you notice about your data? Write down three important things you can say about the data.
1. Most of the numbers have only 1 person in it.
2. No 2 kids chose one number.
3. Lots of people had 102, 101, and 108.

2.37

In preparation for the next Math for All Workshop, please complete the following assignments:

1. Plan and implement a math lesson that supports students' language use.

   - Select a lesson that you will teach before our next workshop. Consult with the colleagues in your team. Read the description of the lesson and enact it with your colleagues (actually do the work of the lesson; don't just think about how it will be done). Analyze the goals and the language demands of the lesson. Take notes in the second column of the Lesson Planning Chart.
   - Think about the strengths and needs of your focal child(ren), and take some notes about how you expect the child or the children to respond to the language demands of the task. Add your notes in the third column of the Lesson Planning Chart (if you need more space, use extra copies of the chart).
   - Together with 2D colleagues in your team, plan some adaptations for the lesson that address the language demands of the student(s). You may want to use Worksheet 2D to think through the suitability of different practices for your focal student(s). Record your ideas in the fourth column of the Lesson Planning chart.
   - Implement the lesson with the adaptations. If possible, invite the members of your team to observe the lesson. (You may want to videotape the focal child so that you and your colleagues can examine him or her as a team.) Have one or more members of your team observe your focal child(ren). Record your observations on the Observation Chart.
   - Answer the Lesson Analysis Questions.

Make sure to bring the completed Learning Goals Worksheet, Lesson Planning Chart, and Observation Chart as well as your answers to the Lesson Analysis Questions to the next workshop session. We may ask you to share your observations and will collect your charts and reflections so we can learn more about the children in our classrooms and your thinking about them. Feel free to submit the Lesson Goals Worksheet and Lesson Planning and Observation Charts as a group. However, please answer the Lesson Analysis Questions individually.

2. Please read one of the following chapters:

   - Chapter 5 ("A Way with Words: Our Language System") from *A Mind at a Time*.
   - Chapter 10 ("Assessing Language") from *Revealing Minds*.

3. Bring curriculum guides and materials for lesson planning.

You will need to use these materials during the workshop to do some planning for a lesson that you will be teaching between the third and fourth workshop sessions. The focus of this planning will be on supporting memory functions. Together with your team, please think of a lesson you might want to focus on. Make sure to bring the curriculum guide for that lesson, and if possible, the manipulatives that go with that lesson to Workshop 3.

WORKSHOP 2   WORKSHEET 2E: LEARNING GOALS

Your Name: _____ Focal Student Pseudonym: _____

Name of the Lesson: _____

Review the introductory pages for the lesson (and its unit) you are planning to help you answer the questions below.

1. What are the learning goals of the lesson?

2. In what ways do you think this lesson connects to what students have studied in math previously (this school year and before)?

3. How do you think what students learn in this lesson will help them with the math they will learn in the future (this school year and beyond)?

WORKSHOP 2 | **WORKSHEET 2F: HANDS-ON EXPLORATION OF THE MATH ACTIVITY**

Read the description of the lesson and enact it with your colleagues. It is important to actually carry out the focal activity of the lesson. Don't just think about how it will be done.

Observe and reflect on what **language functions** you need to use to carry out this activity. Please use the space below to jot down your observations/reflections:

2.40

Your Name: _____

Name of Activity or Lesson Explored: _____

Focal Student Pseudonym: _____

Learning Areas (based on Barringer et al., 2010; Levine, 2002; Pohlman, 2008)	What are the demands of the lesson/activity? What roles do these learning areas play in the lesson activity?	How will the focal child(ren) respond to the demands of the task? Please note strengths and needs below.	How could you change the lesson to make it more accessible to all students, including the focal student(s)?
Language • understands and uses mathematical language (e.g., math vocabulary, concrete and abstract language, contextualized and decontextualized language)			
• using language to communicate with others and to clarify ideas (e.g., understands spoken and written directions, uses spoken and written language to explain one's thinking)			
• using language to develop and master abstract concepts (e.g., verbalizes ideas to push one's thinking, uses language to connect an idea with a visual model)			
• demonstrates higher language function (e.g., understands and uses language that is technical, inferential, symbolic, and abstract)			

Higher Order Thinking • using and forming concepts • solving problems • logical thinking • creative and critical thinking		
Spatial Ordering • interpreting relationships within and between spatial patterns • organizing things in space • reasoning with images		
Sequential Ordering • organizing information in sequence • following directions • managing time		
Memory • short-term memory • active working memory • long-term memory		
Attention • controlling mental energy • maintaining focus • self-monitoring		
Psychosocial • social language • collaboration • conflict resolution		
Motor Coordination • gross motor functions • fine motor functions • grapho-motor functions		

2.42

Language Use and Communication

Your Name: _____   Focal Student Pseudonym: _____

Name of Activity or Lesson Explored: _____

Learning Areas (based on Barringer et al., 2010; Levine, 2002; Pohlman, 2008)	How did the focal student handle the various demands of the activity or lesson? Note your observations below.
Language • understands and uses mathematical language (e.g., math vocabulary, concrete and abstract language, contextualized and decontextualized language)	
• using language to communicate with others and to clarify ideas (e.g., understands spoken and written directions, uses spoken and written language to explain one's thinking)	
• using language to develop and master abstract concepts (e.g., verbalizes ideas to push one's thinking, uses language to connect an idea with a visual model)	
• demonstrates higher language function (e.g., understands and uses language that is technical, inferential, symbolic, and abstract)	
Higher Thinking • using and forming concepts • solving problems • logical thinking • creative and critical thinking	

2.43

Spatial Ordering • interpreting relationships within and between spatial patterns • organizing things in space • reasoning with images				
Sequential Ordering • organizing information in sequence • following directions • managing time				
Memory • short-term memory • active working memory • long-term memory				
Attention • controlling mental energy • maintaining focus • self-monitoring				
Psychosocial • social language • collaboration • conflict resolution				
Motor Coordination • gross motor functions • fine motor functions • grapho-motor functions				

WORKSHOP 2	LESSON ANALYSIS QUESTIONS

Your Name: _____ Focal Student Pseudonym: _____

1. What changes did you and your team make to the original lesson?

2. What do you think students learned? Did they reach the goal(s) of the lesson?

3. Did the students do what you expected them to do? Were there any surprises? Were there any students who didn't participate fully?

4. Did your focal student work as you had hoped he or she would?

5. In what ways did the changes you and your team made to the lesson help the focal student? Did these changes help other students as well?

6. If you were to teach or assist with this lesson again, what would you do differently?

7. How has this assignment influenced your work with students (or teachers)?

Workshop 3

Supporting Memory Functions

WORKSHOP 3   WORKSHOP OVERVIEW

The focus of this workshop session will be on memory functions. Participants will reflect on the role of memory in learning mathematics and learn about the various aspects of memory functions. In the context of a case lesson on finding the factors of 100, participants will analyze the memory demands of the focal activity, which requires students to use coins to model how different factor pairs make $1 (=100 cents). You will observe Luis Carlos, a bilingual student with expressive and receptive language delays, to assess his strengths and needs in memory functions. You will also observe video clips of the teachers teaching the case lesson and reflect on the implementation of specific teaching strategies that support memory functions.

Using the same process as in Workshop 2, you will work in teams to plan memory adaptations for a lesson that you will teach before the next workshop. You should then record and reflect on the implementation of your adaptations and share your experiences at the beginning of Workshop 4.

You will

1. Deepen your understanding of the role of memory functions in mathematics.

2. Learn how to analyze the memory demands of a mathematical task.

3. Learn how to use the neurodevelopmental framework to assess strengths and weaknesses in students' memory functions.

4. Broaden your understanding of specific instructional strategies that support students' memory functions in math.

5. Learn to use their analyses of the neurodevelopmental demands of the task and the strengths and needs of their students to guide planning of adaptations for their math lessons.

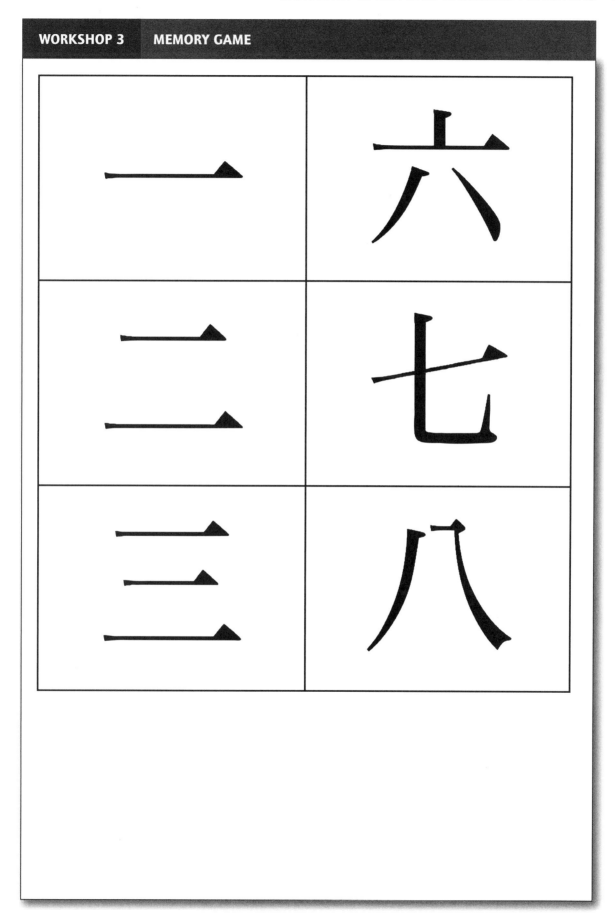

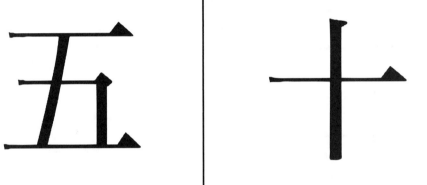

四　九

五　十

一 二 三 四 五 六 七 八 九 十

Use this number line to help you play your game!

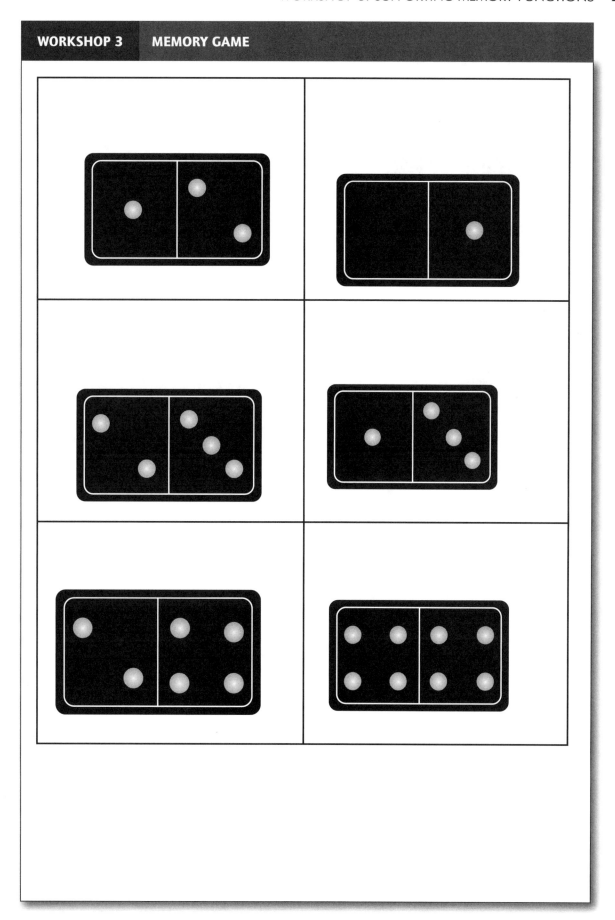

3.4

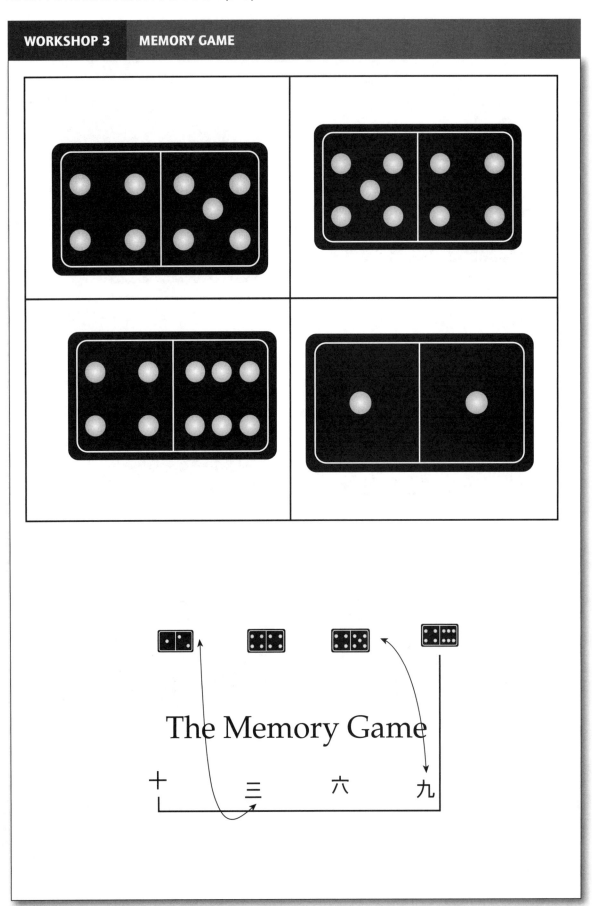

WORKSHOP 3 | **WORKSHEET 3A: HANDS-ON EXPLORATION OF THE MATH ACTIVITY**

Watch the video with the teacher's instructions for the activity. Carry out the activity with your group, following the teacher's instructions.

Observe and reflect on what **memory functions** you need to use to carry out this activity. Please use the space below to jot down your observations/reflections:

3.6

Name of Activity or Lesson Explored: *Dividing a Dollar, 3rd Grade*

Focal Student Pseudonym: *Luis Carlos*

Learning Areas (based on Barringer et al., 2010; Levine, 2002; Pohlman, 2008)	What are the demands of the lesson or activity? What roles do these learning areas play in the *Dividing a Dollar* activity?	How does Luis Carlos respond to the demands of the activity? Please note strengths and needs below.	How did the teachers change the activity, and what teaching practices do they use to make it more accessible to all students, including Luis Carlos? What additional changes would you make?
Memory ***Short-Term Memory*** • recoding information (e.g., paraphrasing, visual images) • processing information from different senses (e.g., visual, verbal, sequential) • use of rehearsal strategies (e.g., forming associations, visualizing, subvocalizing) • rate of processing			
Active Working Memory • combining ideas • combining different parts of an activity • combining short-term memory and long-term memory • combining multiple immediate plans and intentions			
Long-Term Memory • filing (pairs, procedures, categories, rules, and patterns) • access (recall, recognition, automaticity)			

Higher Thinking • using and forming concepts • solving problems • logical thinking • creative and critical thinking				
Language • understanding mathematical language • using language to communicate with others and to clarify one's ideas				
Spatial Ordering • interpreting relationships within and between spatial patterns • organizing things in space • reasoning with images				
Sequential Ordering • organizing information in sequence • following directions • managing time				
Psychosocial • social language • collaboration • conflict resolution				
Attention • controlling mental energy • maintaining focus • self-monitoring				
Motor Coordination • gross motor functions • fine motor functions • grapho-motor functions				

WORKSHOP 3 **WORKSHEET 3C: LEARNING GOALS**

Your Name:_____ Focal Student Pseudonym: _____

Name of the Lesson: _____

Review the introductory pages of the *Dividing a Dollar* lesson for the unit (pages 105 [3.12] to 112 [3.19], and pages 113 [3.20] to 120 [3.27]) to help you answer the questions below.

1. What are the learning goals of the lesson?

2. In what ways do you think this lesson connects to what students have studied in math before (this school year and before)?

3. How do you think what students learn in this lesson will help them with the math they will learn in the future (this school year and beyond)?

3.9

WORKSHEET 3D: TEACHING PRACTICES THAT SUPPORT MEMORY FUNCTIONS

Think about your focal child (or another child from your classroom). Which of the following teaching practices might work for him or her? How would you use these practices?

Teaching Practices	How would you use these practices with your focal student and other students in your classroom?
Make instructions short and say them slowly.	
Preview and review materials to be learned.	
Review concepts and/or skills that were covered in previous class.	
Provide information in manageable units.	
Provide sufficient time for guided practice and independent practice.	
Help students to organize information.	
Have students work with carefully chosen partners.	

WORKSHOP 3	WORKSHEET 3D: TEACHING PRACTICES THAT SUPPORT MEMORY FUNCTIONS

Connect new information to previously known information.	
Make material to be learned meaningful to students, e.g., by actively engaging students, by making connections to real life.	
State connections between math topics explicitly.	
Give cues to make students aware of important information.	
Use multiple representations to teach a concept.	
Help children organize their workspace.	

Unit Guide for "Dividing a Dollar" Lesson

UNIT OVERVIEW

Landmarks in the Hundreds

Content of This Unit   Students work with 100, factors of 100, and multiples of 100 (up to 1000). They use coins, 100 charts, and cubes to investigate these numbers. They develop a sense of these quantities by counting real objects and by making "pictures" of 100 and 1000. They develop their own strategies, based on what they know about these landmark numbers, to solve multiplication and division problems.

Connections with Other Units   If you are doing the full-year *Investigations* curriculum in the suggested sequence for grade 3, this is the fifth of ten units. Your class will have already completed the Multiplication and Division unit *Things That Come in Groups.* There, students practiced skip counting by 2's, 3's, 4's, 5's, and 6's, and worked on such problems as "how many 4's in 48?" If your students have not had comparable experience, spend more time on the first three sessions of Investigation 1. During Investigation 2, these students may also need to spend more time working with multiples of 10 and with the smaller multiples of 100.

If your school is not using the full-year curriculum, this unit can also be used successfully at grade 4. The work in this unit is continued and extended in the grade 4–5 unit, *Landmarks in the Thousands.*

Investigations Curriculum ■ Suggested Grade 3 Sequence

Mathematical Thinking at Grade 3 (Introduction)

Things That Come in Groups (Multiplication and Division)

Flips, Turns, and Area (2-D Geometry)

From Paces to Feet (Measuring and Data)

▶ *Landmarks in the Hundreds* (The Number System)

Up and Down the Number Line (Changes)

Combining and Comparing (Addition and Subtraction)

Turtle Paths (2-D Geometry)

Fair Shares (Fractions)

Exploring Solids and Boxes (3-D Geometry)

Investigation 1 ▪ Finding Factors

Class Sessions	Activities	Pacing
Session 1 (p. 4) SKIP COUNTING WITH CUBES	Ways to Count to 10 Finding Factors with Cubes Homework: Ways to Make _____	minimum 1 hr
Sessions 2 and 3 (p. 7) FACTORS OF 24, 36, AND 48	Skip Counting on the 100 Chart What's a Factor? Making Counting Charts for 24 Factors of 36 and 48 Teacher Checkpoint: Showing Factors of 36 or 48 Class Discussion: What Did You Find Out About 24, 36, and 48? Homework: Factors of 36/Factors of 48	minimum 2 hr
Sessions 4 and 5 (p. 17) FACTORS OF 100	What Numbers Are Factors of 100? Making a Picture of 100 Homework: A Picture of 100	minimum 2 hr
Sessions 6 and 7 (p. 22) DIVIDING A DOLLAR	Listing the Factors of 100 Working with Coins Dividing a Dollar Among Five People How Can We Divide a Dollar Evenly? Teacher Checkpoint: Factors of 100 Homework: Share a Dollar	minimum 2 hr

◔ Ten-Minute Math ▪ Counting Around the Class

Mathematical Emphasis

- Understanding the relationship between skip counting and grouping (for example, as we count 3, 6, 9, 12, we are adding a group of 3 to the total each time)

- Becoming familiar with the relationships among commonly encountered factors and multiples (for example, is 3 a factor of 24? How many 3's does it take to make 24?)

- Increasing fluency in counting by single-digit numbers (2's, 3's, 4's, 6's, 8's) as well as by useful two-digit numbers (10's, 20's, 25's)

- Developing familiarity with the factors of 100, an important landmark in our number system, and their relationships to 100 through work with cubes, coins, and 100 charts

Assessment Resources

Teacher Checkpoint: Showing Factors of 36 or 48 (p. 12)

Students' Problems with Skip Counting (Teacher Note, p. 14)

Teacher Checkpoint: Factors of 100 (p. 27)

Materials

Snap™ Cubes

Overhead projector and transparencies

Colored paper

Scissors

Glue or paste

Crayons or markers

Scrap materials

Plastic or real coins

Student Sheets 1–10

Teaching resource sheets

Family letter

Two Ways to Count to Ten, retold by Ruby Dee (opt.)

Unit Overview ▪ **I-13**

3.13

Investigation 2 ▪ Using Landmarks to Solve Problems

Class Sessions	Activities	Pacing
Sessions 1, 2, and 3 (p. 32) MOVING BEYOND 100	Hundreds from Home Choice Time: Exploring Multiples of 100 Class Discussion: Finding Patterns in the 20's Assessment: How Many in 500? Homework: Money Problems Homework: Skip Counting Homework: How Many 4's Are in 600?	minimum 3 hr
Session 4 (p. 41) SOLVING PROBLEMS WITH MONEY	Class Discussion: Six People Paying $1.50 Each Problems Using Money Homework: More Money Problems	minimum 1 hr
Sessions 5 and 6 (p. 44) REAL-WORLD MULTIPLYING AND DIVIDING	Using Standard Notation for Division Choice Time: Working with Landmarks Multiplying and Dividing on the Calculator Homework: Multiplying Things at Home Homework: Making Up Landmark Problems Extension: Things That Number in the Low Hundreds Extension: Things That Number in the High Hundreds Extension: Exploring Different Calculators	minimum 2 hr

◔ Ten-Minute Math ▪ Calendar Math

Mathematical Emphasis

- Using knowledge about factors of 100 to understand the structure of multiples of 100 (if there are four 25's in 100, there are twelve 25's in 300)

- Developing strategies to solve problems in multiplication and division situations by using knowledge of factors and multiples

- Estimating real quantities that are close to 200, 300, and 400

- Reading and using standard multiplication and division notation to record problems and answers

Assessment Resources

Assessment: How Many in 500? (Teacher Note, p. 37)

Hundreds from Home (Dialogue Box, p. 39)

How Many 20's in 280? (Dialogue Box, p. 40)

Using Multiples to Count (Teacher Note, p. 49)

Talking and Writing About Division (Teacher Note, p. 50)

Materials

Snap™ Cubes

Plastic or real coins

Calculators

Students' "Pictures of 100"

Overhead projector

Student Sheets 11–16

Teaching resource sheets

Investigation 3 ▪ Constructing a 1000 Chart

Class Sessions	Activities	Pacing
Session 1 (p. 54) A 1000 CHART	Making a Thousand Homework: More Than 300	minimum 1 hr
Sessions 2 and 3 (p. 56) FINDING LARGE QUANTITIES	Locating Numbers on the 1000 Chart Finding Real Quantities for the 1000 Chart Assessment: Calculating with the 1000 Chart Choosing Student Work to Save	minimum 2 hr

◔ **Ten-Minute Math ▪ Counting Around the Class**

Mathematical Emphasis

- Using factors of 100 to understand the structure of 1000 (How many 50's does it take to make 1000?)

- Estimating quantities up to 1000 (What can we find in the classroom that numbers about 500?)

- Using landmarks to calculate "distances" within 1000 (How far is it from 650 to 950?)

Assessment Resources

Assessment: Calculating with the 1000 Chart (p. 58)

Assessment: How Far from 650 to 1000? (Teacher Note, p. 59)

Choosing Student Work to Save (p. 59)

Materials

Large poster or chart paper

Scissors

Glue or tape

Crayons or markers

Small counters or cubes

String or ribbon (opt.)

Snap™ Cubes

Plastic or real coins

Calculators

Teaching resource sheets

Student Sheet 17

WORKSHOP 3 | **LESSON MATERIALS**

MATERIALS LIST

Following are the basic materials needed for the activities in this unit.

- Snap™ Cubes (interlocking cubes): at least 50 per pair of students

- Plastic coins: at least 50 pennies, 25 nickels, 12 dimes, and 6 quarters per small group of students (real coins may be substituted or used in addition to these)

- Calculators: at least 1 per pair of students

- Small counters or cubes (1 cm): 1 per student

- *Two Ways to Count to Ten*, retold by Ruby Dee (optional)

- Large poster or chart paper: 1 sheet per pair of students

- Colored paper

- Scrap materials

- Scissors

- Glue or paste

- Tape

- Crayons or markers

- String or ribbon (optional)

- Overhead projector

The following materials are provided at the end of this unit as blackline masters. A Student Activity Booklet containing all student sheets and teaching resources needed for individual work is available.

Family Letter (p. 68)

Student Sheets 1–17 (p. 69)

Teaching Resources:

    Money Problems (p. 85)

    More Money Problems (p. 86)

    Division Problems (p. 87)

    One-Centimeter Graph Paper (p. 89)

    100 Chart (p. 90)

    300 Chart (p. 91)

Practice Pages (p. 93)

Related Children's Literature

Dee, Ruby. *Two Ways to Count to Ten*. New York: Henry Holt, 1988.

Kasza, Keiko. *The Wolf's Chicken Stew*. New York: G. P. Putnam, 1987.

Silverstein, Shel. "Smart" in *Where the Sidewalk Ends*. New York: Harper and Row, 1974.

Viorst, Judith. *Alexander, Who Used to Be Rich Last Sunday*. New York: Atheneum, 1978.

I-16 ▪ *Landmarks in the Hundreds*

Note: The blackline masters for this unit are not included in this book.

ABOUT THE MATHEMATICS IN THIS UNIT

An important part of students' mathematical work in the elementary grades is building an understanding of the base ten number system. This unit provides activities that develop knowledge about important *landmarks* in that system—numbers that are familiar landing places, that make for simple calculations, and to which other numbers can be related.

Because our number system is based on powers of ten, the numbers 10, 100, 1000, and their multiples are especially important landmarks. In solving real problems, people with well-developed number sense draw on their knowledge of these important landmarks. For example, think about how you would solve this problem, in your head, before you continue reading:

> If there are about 25 students in a class and 17 classes in our school, about how many students are there altogether?

Many people would use their knowledge that there are four 25's in every 100 to help them solve this problem mentally. Rather than multiplying 17 by 25, they will think something like this: "Four 25's in 100, eight in 200, 12, 16, that's 400, and one more 25 makes 425."

Knowledge about 10, 100, 1000, their multiples, and their factors is the basis of good number sense. As students learn about 100, how to take it apart into its factors, and how to use it to construct other numbers, they gain the knowledge they need to develop their own strategies to solve problems using quantities in the hundreds. They develop good estimation strategies and are less likely to make the kinds of errors that result from the use of faulty algorithms.

For example, a student who has developed knowledge about 20 and its relationship to 100, who has experience counting by 20's, and knows what the pattern of the multiples of 20 is like, would never make this common error:

$$\begin{array}{r} 440 \\ -\ 380 \\ \hline 140 \end{array}$$

Using a written subtraction algorithm—whether faulty or correct—is not a sensible approach to solving this problem. Rather, by inspecting the numbers and using knowledge of important landmarks in the number system, students should eventually be able to solve this problem mentally with no trouble:

> "380 to 400 is 20, then 20, 40, two more 20's gets to 440, so that's three 20's. The answer is 60."

Mathematical Emphasis At the beginning of each investigation, the Mathematical Emphasis section tells you what is most important for students to learn about during that investigation. Many of these mathematical understandings and processes are difficult and complex. Students gradually learn more and more about each idea over many years of schooling. Individual students will begin and end the unit with different levels of knowledge and skill, but all will gain greater knowledge about 100 and multiples of 100 and develop strategies for solving problems involving these important numbers.

ABOUT THE ASSESSMENT IN THIS UNIT

Throughout the *Investigations* curriculum, there are many opportunities for ongoing daily assessment as you observe, listen to, and interact with students at work. In this unit, you will find two Teacher Checkpoints:

Investigation 1, Sessions 2–3:
Showing Factors of 36 or 48 (p. 12)

Investigation 1, Sessions 6–7:
Factors of 100 (p. 27)

This unit also has two embedded Assessment activities:

Investigation 2, Sessions 1–3:
How Many in 500? (p. 36)

Investigation 3, Sessions 2–3:
Calculating with the 1000 Chart (p. 58)

In addition, you can use almost any activity in this unit to assess your students' needs and strengths. Listed below are questions to help you focus your observation. You may want to keep track of your observations for each student to help you plan your curriculum and monitor students' growth. Suggestions for documenting student growth can be found in the section About Assessment (p. I–10).

Investigation 1: Finding Factors

■ How do students use cubes to count to 20? 36? 48? How do they arrange the cubes when they look for factors? How do they predict how many groups of a factor it will take to make 20? 36? 48? etc.? How do students make use of skip counting in looking for factors?

■ Do students understand the relationship between factors and multiples? How do they transform a statement about factors to one about multiples?

■ How do children show their fluency with skip counting? Are their strategies different when counting by two-digit numbers?

■ What strategies do children use to predict how many 4's or 20's are in 100? How do they present their conclusions?

Investigation 2: Using Landmarks to Solve Problems

■ How do students figure out how many groups of a certain number are in a collection of 100 objects? How do they use this knowledge to make predictions about 200 and 300? How do they use this information to predict how many of that particular factor will be in higher numbers such as 500? In in-between numbers such as 640?

■ How do students use information about factors and multiples in doing multiplication and division problems? Can they use what they know about 100 to figure out 500 divided by 25? Or 25 × 9?

■ How do students use estimating strategies and knowledge of landmark numbers, factors, and multiples to help them find groups of equal size that total in the hundreds? Can they extend their strategies to 200's, 300's, and 400's?

■ Do students recognize, interpret, and use standard forms and symbols for multiplication and division? Can they do this both on paper and when using the calculator? How do they interpret a problem that is presented in a variety of ways, including standard notation?

Investigation 3: Constructing a 1000 Chart

■ How do children figure out how many graph paper squares there are on their partially completed 1000 charts? How do they figure out how many more groups of 20's, 25's, or 100's they need to complete their chart? How do they locate multiples of 100 on their 1000 chart? Multiples of factors they have been using?

■ What strategies do students use to locate quantities of items that are greater than 300? Around 1000? How do students find the corresponding numbers on the 1000 chart? What counting or grouping methods do they use to check if their estimate is accurate?

■ How do students make use of landmark numbers when finding distances on the 1000 chart? Do they see the relationships between addition and subtraction? multiplication and division?

Assessment Sourcebook

In the *Assessment Sourcebook* you will find End-of-Unit Assessment Tasks and Assessment Masters available in English and Spanish. You will also find suggestions to help you observe and evaluate student work and checklists of mathematical emphases with space for you to record individual student information.

PREVIEW FOR THE LINGUISTICALLY DIVERSE CLASSROOM

In the *Investigations* curriculum, mathematical vocabulary is introduced naturally during the activities. We don't ask students to learn definitions of new terms; rather, they come to understand such words as *factor* or *area* or *symmetry* by hearing them used frequently in discussion as they investigate new concepts. This approach is compatible with current theories of second-language acquisition, which emphasize the use of new vocabulary in meaningful contexts while students are actively involved with objects, pictures, and physical movement.

Listed below are some key words used in this unit that will not be new to most English speakers at this age level, but may be unfamiliar to students with limited English proficiency. You will want to spend additional time working on these words with your students who are learning English. If your students are working with a second-language teacher, you might enlist your colleague's aid in familiarizing students with these words, before and during this unit. In the classroom, look for opportunities for students to hear and use these words. Activities you can use to present the words are given in the appendix, Vocabulary Support for Second-Language Learners (p. 65).

the numbers 1 to 100   Students use the 100 chart throughout the unit. They should be able to write the numerals and identify each by name.

divide, group, equal, unequal   As students learn about factors in this unit, they *divide* collections of cubes or amounts of money into *equal groups*.

money: coins, cents, nickel, dime, quarter, dollar   In order to "divide a dollar evenly among five people," students need to recognize U.S. coins and know the value of each.

pattern   Finding patterns is a key mathematical process. In this unit, students look for visual patterns on the 100 chart (for example, the diagonal pattern created when skip counting by 3's) and for number patterns (for example, when counting by 5's, alternating numbers end in 5 and 0).

Multicultural Extensions for All Students

Whenever possible, encourage students to share words, objects, customs, or any aspects of daily life from their own cultures and backgrounds that are relevant to the activities in this unit. For example:

- Students who have coins from their countries of origin can bring them to show to the class. They might make a poster showing equivalencies of the coins in these monetary systems.

- When students are making up their own word problems, encourage them to write problems that are based on aspects of their cultures— foods, games and sports that involve teams, and so forth.

Preview for the Linguistically Diverse Classroom ▪ **I-19**

Sessions 6 and 7

Dividing a Dollar

Materials

- Interlocking cubes
- 100 charts
- Sample coin collections in differing total amounts (48 to 60 cents) for each pair
- A container of coins for each small group (at least 50 pennies, 25 nickels, 12 dimes, 6 quarters)
- Student Sheet 9 (1 per student)
- Student Sheet 10 (1 per student, homework)
- Overhead projector

What Happens

The class lists and discusses all the factors of 100 they have found. Students use coins to explore how to share a dollar equally among five people, then investigate ways to divide a dollar evenly among different numbers of people. Their work focuses on:

- continuing to explore which numbers are and are not factors of 100, using money as a context
- continuing to become familiar with how many of a certain factor make 100 (for example, that four 25's make 100), in the context of money
- determining the value of a collection of coins

 Ten-Minute Math: Counting Around the Class In short sessions at various times during the day, continue to do Counting Around the Class as described in Sessions 4 and 5. Try counting by 10's. For other variations, see p. 61.

Activity

Listing the Factors of 100

Work with students to make a large class chart of all the factors of 100, based on their work in the preceding sessions. You'll need to make a chart that can remain posted. Have students help you list these factors from the least to the greatest. Ask:

Do you think we have all the factors of 100? Why do you think so? Are there any numbers you didn't try that might work?

Then add to the chart how many of each factor it takes to make 100, asking students to supply these numbers:

How many 20's make 100? How do you know? Who can prove it a different way? How many 2's make 100? How do you know? Who has a different way to explain the solution?

Encourage students to refer to their work with cubes and 100 charts as ways to explain what they think. For example:

> When I did it with cubes, we did it in 20's, and we needed 5 rows of 20's.
>
> I can tell it's five 20's because I counted on the 100 chart—20, 40, 60, 80, 100, that's five.

Add these results, with the associated words and multiplication equations, to your chart. Include only the factors your students have found.

Factor of 100	*How many make 100?*	*Say it in words*	*Say it as an equation*
1	100	100 groups of 1	$100 \times 1 = 100$
2	50	50 groups of 2	$50 \times 2 = 100$
4	25	25 groups of 4	$25 \times 4 = 100$
5	20	20 groups of 5	$20 \times 5 = 100$
10	10	10 groups of 10	$10 \times 10 = 100$
20	5	5 groups of 20	$5 \times 20 = 100$
25	4	4 groups of 25	$4 \times 25 = 100$
50	2	2 groups of 50	$2 \times 50 = 100$
100	1	1 group of 100	$1 \times 100 = 100$

Ask students what they notice about the list. Someone may notice related pairs; for example, they may see 20 groups of 5 and 5 groups of 20 (or, two 50's and fifty 2's). If no student notices this, you might point out one of the matching pairs yourself. This discussion can lead students to identify factors that are not yet on their list. Those students who have already worked with arrays in the Multiplication and Division unit, *Things That Come in Groups*, may be able to describe why they think both pairs work.

If the chart is not yet complete, or if your students are not sure whether they have all the factors, tell them that you will keep the chart posted and add to it if they find more factors. You may also want to post miniature 100 charts showing the pattern for each factor.

WORKSHOP 3 | **LESSON GUIDE FOR "DIVIDING A DOLLAR" LESSON**

Activity

Working with Coins

Give pairs of students the small sample coin collections (a few pennies, nickels, dimes, and at least one quarter, in differing amounts from about 48 to 60 cents). Review the values of coins with your class:

What is a nickel worth? A dime? A dime and a nickel together? How do you know? What is a quarter plus a nickel worth? How do you know? Which is the biggest coin? How much is it worth? Is the smallest coin worth the smallest amount of money?

❖ **Tip for the Linguistically Diverse Classroom** Reword questions so that students can respond nonverbally. For example:

Show me a coin that is worth 5 cents.

Show me a coin that is worth 10 cents.

Show me two coins that equal 30 cents.

Ask each pair to figure out how much money they have altogether. You may want to have each pair trade its coin collection with another pair and calculate the new total.

Have one pair tell how many of each coin is in their collection. Draw these on the board or put them on the overhead. Ask the class to come up with different counting strategies for figuring out the total.

Note: Each day you use money, students enjoy finding out how much their collection is worth before doing other activities. This provides for good practice in counting by 5's, 10's, and 25's. It also allows students to check their collection at the end of class to make sure they have the same total before putting their coins away.

Activity

Dividing a Dollar Among Five People

We're going to be finding out more about 100 by using money. If I had a dollar in pennies, how many pennies would I have?

Establish that there are 100 pennies or 100 cents in a dollar.

We're going to work on how we can split up 100 pennies evenly. If I had a dollar, could I share it equally between Midori and Chantelle? How much would each person get?

Students will probably know how to divide a dollar in half. Hold a short discussion of how much each person would get and how the students know that. What coins could they use to make this amount?

Give each small group their container of additional coins, and pose the following problem for work in pairs or small groups:

Now, could I split a dollar equally among Midori, Chantelle, Sean, Michael, and Khanh? How much would each person get? Find as many different ways as possible that you could divide a dollar equally among five people.

In this activity, giving two dimes to each person is considered different from giving four nickels to each person. You can clarify this as you circulate. Once students have one solution, you can explain what a "different solution" is by saying something like this:

Suppose you didn't have enough dimes to give everyone two dimes. Could you use some different coins to give each person an equal amount?

Recording and Sharing Solutions Students work in small groups, recording each way they find so that they can remember and report their solutions later. They might use pictures, words, symbols, or a combination of these. We have deliberately not provided a student sheet for recording their findings, so that students can devise their own way of recording their solutions. As you circulate, remind students to record each solution with words, numbers, or pictures.

Try to interpret their recording. If it is unclear, insist that they clarify:

I can tell that you used nickels, but I don't understand how many nickels each person would get.

After a while, have groups share their answers with the whole class. Ask each group to share a *new* method—one that has not yet been shown by someone else. To share their solution, they might specify in a sentence what each person gets, or they might arrange the coins on the overhead projector. You might want to keep a chart of their findings.

Your students may not realize at first that every solution they find involves giving 20 cents to each person. The **Dialogue Box**, Dividing a Dollar Among Five People (p. 28), illustrates how one pair discovered that they always had to use 20 cents.

Sessions 6 and 7: Dividing a Dollar ▪ **25**

3.23

WORKSHOP 3   **LESSON GUIDE FOR "DIVIDING A DOLLAR" LESSON**

Activity

How Can We Divide a Dollar Evenly?

Dividing a Dollar Among Three People   Pose the following question to the whole class:

Could you share a dollar equally among three people—Latisha, Mark, and Samir? How could you do it?

> There is a way, but it wouldn't be a fair way. Someone would have 34 cents and the rest 33 cents.

After sharing a dollar among two and five people, students may think that it is possible to split a dollar among any number of people. Trying to split a dollar among three people, however, will be puzzling to many.

One approach to this discussion is to put 10 towers of 10 cubes each on the overhead. Ask students what they would do to divide these "pennies" up among three people. See the **Dialogue Box**, 100 Cents and 3 People (p. 29), for part of a discussion that occurred in one classroom.

If this problem remains puzzling to some, leave it as an open question for students to continue exploring, working with coins or cubes in their groups.

How Can You Split a Dollar Evenly?   Review the class findings so far about how a dollar can be divided evenly. Start a class chart, as shown. Include numbers of people the students know cannot divide a dollar evenly.

Students may know some other numbers they can add to the chart; for example, that 10 people would each get 10 cents, or that 99 people cannot divide a dollar evenly. If students give such information, add it to the chart.

Students then work in pairs to find out what other numbers of people could share a dollar equally. Hand out Student Sheet 9, Ways to Split Up a Dollar, for their recording. To get students started, suggest that they choose one or two of the following to explore: 4 people, 8 people, 25 people, 50 people, or 30 people.

Number of people sharing a dollar	How much each gets
2 people	50¢
5 people	20¢
Cannot split a dollar evenly	
3 people	

26 ▪ *Investigation 1: Finding Factors*

They may also choose other numbers that interest them. Some students will work on just one or two of these problems. Others may become interested in finding all the possible ways to divide a dollar evenly. In either case, it's important that each student be able to describe and justify his or her solutions.

Some students may come up with solutions that don't involve whole cents, for example, giving each of three people 33 1/3 cents. This is a good opportunity to talk about fractions of wholes and for the class to see and interpret fraction notation. Acknowledge that such an answer is an interesting mathematical solution, but that it would be impossible to actually give anyone 1/3 of a cent. You may also want to make a separate category on your class list: "Solutions that work with numbers, but not with pennies."

Number of people sharing a dollar	How much each gets
2 people	50¢
4 people	25¢
5 people	20¢
10 people	10¢
20 people	5¢
100 people	1¢

Cannot split a dollar evenly
3 people
8 people
anything over 50

Summing Up   Add student findings to your class chart.

Activity

By this time, students should be quite familiar with the factors of 100. This is a good time to pause and make sure that your students are comfortable with the relationships between 100 and its factors, before you go on to work with higher numbers. Pose these two questions (write them on the board or overhead):

Teacher Checkpoint
Factors of 100

How many 20's are in 100?
How many 4's are in 100?

Ask students to find the answers to these and to prove their solutions using coins, cubes, or 100 charts, then write or draw explanations of their solutions. The purpose of their writing and drawing is to demonstrate convincingly that their solution is correct. If you are keeping student portfolios, this piece of work could be one to save.

> There are 25 4's in 100.
>
> I counted by 4 on the 100 chart.
>
> I found 25 4's in a zig zag line.

There may be some students who need more work with 100. When you go on to work with multiples of 100 in Investigation 2, you can adjust the numbers for those students. Thus, instead of finding how many 25's in 200 and 300, they might find how many 10's in 70, 80, and 90; how many 20's in 40, 60, and 80; and so forth.

Sessions 6 and 7 Follow-Up

Share a Dollar   Send home Student Sheet 10, Share a Dollar. Students try to find a way to share $1.00 among 10 people. Then they make up their own share-a-dollar problem and solve it. You may want to allow time for them to solve one another's problems during class.

 **Homework**

Dividing a Dollar Among Five People

This discussion between two students takes place while they are working together on the activity Dividing a Dollar Among Five People (p. 24).

See how you could share a dollar equally among five people. I want you to find as many combinations as possible.

[*Yoshi and Amanda are working together. Amanda lines up 5 dimes.*]

Yoshi: We found one—two dimes!

Amanda: Wait, I'm not sure yet. [*She adds a second dime on top of each of the first 5.*]

Yoshi [*impatiently*]: That's it!

Amanda [*not yet satisfied*]: We need to check it. Fifty plus fifty ... yes.

Yoshi [*already onto another solution*]: They could each get 4 nickels ... it's the same thing!

[*Amanda begins to try nickels, making piles of 4.*]

Amanda: I don't know if we've got enough to do it.

Yoshi: Yes, 4 nickels is the same thing. And we could use 20 pennies, it's the same thing. It works.

[*Amanda, working on a solution independently, places 1 dime and 2 nickels in each of five piles.*]

Amanda [*counting the dimes first*]: 10, 20, 30, 40, 50 ... [*then the nickels*] 55, 60, 65, 70, 75, 80, 85, 90, 95, 100. [*She then tries groups of 5 nickels.*]

Yoshi: That's too many.

Amanda: No, wait, I want to try it! Don't worry, I know what I'm doing.

[*Amanda counts her nickels by fives. After the fourth pile, her count is already up to $1.00, with 5 nickels left, so she abandons this idea.*]

Amanda: Let's think of another one not using 20 cents. [*Pause.*] No, we have to use 20 cents, don't we?

Yoshi: We could do 10 pennies and 2 nickels, that would work.

[*Amanda again gets the coins to try it, as she is not convinced without using the coins.*]

28 ■ *Investigation 1: Finding Factors*

3.26

D I A L O G U E   B O X

100 Cents and 3 People

This class discussion takes place during the activity How Can We Divide a Dollar Evenly? (p. 26).

Could you share a dollar equally among three people? How would you do it?

Elena: 30 pennies.

Dylan: That equals 90.

[*The teacher puts three groups of 30 on the overhead.*]

How about these 10 left over?

Ricardo: I think you should put them in 20's.

[*The teacher puts out three groups of 20.*]

Ricardo: Give 10 to the 20's.

Su-Mei: It still equals 90.

Aaron: I don't see any way … I don't think you could do it.

Yoshi: 34.

So keep these 30's and add 4 more to each? What do you think is going to happen then?

Latisha: Two cents will get left over. You'll get 4 and 4 each and that's 8, and 8 from 10 is 2, so there's 2 left over.

Sean: I think 2's would work. No, do it by 1's.

Jamal: I think if you gave 33 each, you'd have one left over and you could divide it into thirds, if you had a butcher knife or something.

Tamara: It's impossible to divide 10 into three because 10 is an even number and 3 is an odd number, and you can't divide 10 into 3 equal groups.

Aaron: 33 plus 33 plus 33 equals 99, so how can you make 100?

Ricardo: I think if you take all those 30's and make 'em into 20's, it would work.

Jennifer: If you start with 5's, it might do it.

By the end of this discussion, some students believed that there is no solution with whole cents, while others were still convinced that sharing in the right way might make it possible to divide $1.00 in three ways evenly.

Students then worked with interlocking cubes to model this problem. Those who were pretty sure that there was no way to divide $1.00 evenly among three people enjoyed proving their solution with the cubes, while students who were unconvinced by the group discussion needed to work with the cubes themselves.

Tamara's conjecture, "You can't divide an even number by an odd number," is an idea that often comes up in this discussion. While Tamara is right that you can't divide 10 into three equal groups, her generalization does not hold up—for example, you can divide 10 by five. If this idea comes up in your class, you might want to list the conjecture somewhere, ask students to think about it, and discuss it further when students work on division problems later in the unit: "Can we ever divide an even number by an odd number? an odd number by an even number?"

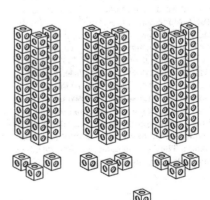

WORKSHOP 3	HOMEWORK ASSIGNMENT

In preparation for our next Math for All Workshop, please complete the following assignments:

1. Plan and implement a math lesson that supports students' memory functions.

   - Select a lesson that you will teach before our next workshop. Consult with the colleagues in your team. Read the description of the lesson and enact it with your colleagues (actually do the work of the lesson; don't just think about how it will be done). Analyze the goals and the memory demands of the lesson. Take notes in the second column of the Lesson Planning Chart.
   - Think about the strengths and needs of one or more focal children, and take some notes about how you expect the child or the children to respond to the memory demands of the task. Add your notes in the third column of the Lesson Planning Chart (if you need more space, use extra copies of the chart).
   - Together with the colleagues in your team, plan some adaptations for the lesson. Record your ideas in the fourth column of the Lesson Planning chart.
   - Implement the lesson with the adaptations. If possible, invite the members of your team to observe the lesson. (You may want to videotape the focal child so that you and your colleagues can examine him or her as a team.) Have one or more members of your team observe your focal child(ren). Record your observations on the Observation Chart.
   - Answer the Lesson Analysis Questions.
   - Make sure to bring the completed Learning Goals Worksheet, Lesson Planning Chart, and Observation Chart as well as your answers to the *Lesson Analysis Questions* to the next workshop session. We may ask you to share your observations and will collect your charts and reflections so we can learn more about the children in your classrooms and your thinking about them. Feel free to submit the Lesson Goals worksheet and Lesson Planning and Observation Charts as a group. However, please answer the Lesson Analysis Questions individually.

2. Please read one of the following chapters:

   - Chapter 4 ("Remembering to Learn and Learning to Remember") from *A Mind at a Time*.
   - Chapter 9 ("Assessing Memory") from *Revealing Minds*.

3. Bring curriculum guides and materials for lesson planning.

   - You will need to use these materials during the workshop to do some planning for a lesson that you will be teaching between the fourth and fifth workshop sessions. The focus of this planning will be on supporting collaborative group work. Together with your team, please think of a lesson you might want to focus on. Make sure to bring the curriculum guide for that lesson, and if possible, the manipulatives that go with it to our next workshop.

WORKSHOP 3	WORKSHEET 3E: LEARNING GOALS

Your Name: _____ Focal Student Pseudonym: _____

Name of the Lesson: _____

Review the introductory pages for the lesson (and its unit) you are planning to help you answer the questions below.

1. What are the learning goals of the lesson?

2. In what ways do you think this lesson connects to what students have studied in math before (this school year and before)?

3. How do you think what students learn in this lesson will help them with the math they will learn in the future (this school year and beyond)?

3.29

WORKSHOP 3   **WORKSHEET 3F: HANDS-ON EXPLORATION OF THE MATH ACTIVITY**

Read the description of the lesson and enact it with your colleagues. It is important to actually carry out the focal activity of the lesson. Don't just think about how it will be done.

Observe and reflect on what *memory functions* you need to use to carry out this activity. Please use the space below to jot down your observations/reflections:

Your Name: _____

Name of Activity or Lesson Explored: _____   Focal Student Pseudonym: _____

Learning Areas (based on Barringer et al., 2010; Levine, 2002; Pohlman, 2008)	What are the demands of the lesson or activity? What roles do these learning areas play in the activity or lesson?	How will the focal child(ren) respond to the demands of the activity? Please note strengths and needs below.	How could you change the lesson to make it more accessible to all students, including the focal student(s)?
Memory *Short-Term Memory* • recoding information (e.g., paraphrasing, visual images) • processing information from different senses (e.g., visual, verbal, sequential) • use of rehearsal strategies (e.g., forming associations, visualizing, subvocalizing) • rate of processing			
Active Working Memory • combining ideas • combining different parts of an activity • combining short-term memory and long-term memory • combining multiple immediate plans and intentions			
Long-Term Memory • filing (pairs, procedures, categories, rules, and patterns) • access (recall, recognition, automaticity)			
Higher Thinking • using and forming concepts • solving problems • logical thinking • creative and critical thinking			

3.31

Language • understanding mathematical language • using language to communicate with others and to clarify one's ideas **Ordering** *Spatial* • interpreting relationships within and between spatial patterns • organizing things in space • reasoning with images **Ordering** *Sequential* • organizing information in sequence • following directions • managing time **Psychosocial** • social language • collaboration • conflict resolution **Attention** • controlling mental energy • maintaining focus • self-monitoring **Motor Coordination** • gross motor functions • fine motor functions • grapho-motor functions					

Memory Functions

Your Name: _____

Name of Activity or Lesson Explored: _____

Focal Student Pseudonym: _____

Learning Areas (based on Barringer et al., 2010; Levine, 2002; Pohlman, 2008)	How did the focal student handle the various demands of the activity or lesson? Note your observations below.
Memory	
Short-Term Memory	
• recoding information (e.g., paraphrasing, visual images)	
• processing information from different senses (e.g., visual, verbal, sequential)	
• use of rehearsal strategies (e.g., forming associations, visualizing, subvocalizing)	
• rate of processing	
Active Working Memory	
• combining ideas	
• combining different parts of an activity	
• combining short-term memory and long-term memory	
• combining multiple immediate plans and intentions	
Long-Term Memory	
• filing (pairs, procedures, categories, rules, and patterns)	
• access (recall, recognition, automaticity)	
Higher Thinking	
• using and forming concepts	
• solving problems	
• logical thinking	
• creative and critical thinking	

Language

- understanding mathematical language
- using language to communicate with others and to clarify one's ideas

Spatial Ordering

- interpreting relationships within and between spatial patterns
- organizing things in space
- reasoning with images

Sequential

- organizing information in sequence
- following directions
- managing time

Psychosocial

- social language
- collaboration
- conflict resolution

Attention

- controlling mental energy
- maintaining focus
- self-monitoring

Motor Coordination

- gross motor functions
- fine motor functions
- grapho-motor functions

WORKSHOP 3	REFLECTION QUESTIONS

Your Name: _____ Focal Student Pseudonym: _____

1. What changes did you and your team make to the original lesson?

2. What do you think students learned? Did they reach the goal(s) of the lesson?

3. Did the students do what you expected them to do? Were there any surprises? Were there any students who didn't participate fully?

4. Did your focal student work as you had hoped he or she would?

5. In what ways did the changes you and your team made to the lesson help the focal student? Did these changes help other students as well?

6. If you were to teach or assist with this lesson again, what would you do differently?

7. How has this assignment influenced your work with students (or teachers)?

3.35

Workshop 4

Supporting Psychosocial Functions

This workshop will focus in-depth on psychosocial functions. You will discuss the role of social behavior and social language in learning mathematics and learn how the neurodevelopmental framework describes the components of psychosocial functions. A third-grade lesson on geometry serves as the case lesson for this workshop. You will analyze the psychosocial demands of one of the focal activities of this lesson, which requires children to work in pairs to find the lines of symmetry of various geometric shapes. You will view video of Shamira, a student who has difficulties with receptive language, to assess her strengths and needs in psychosocial functions in this activity. You will then consider how different kinds of instructional strategies could be used to support psychosocial functions in this lesson.

Using the same process as in Workshops 2 and 3, participants will work in teams to plan psychosocial adaptations for a lesson that they will teach before the next workshop. Participants will record and reflect on the implementation of their adaptations and share their experiences at the beginning of Workshop 5.

You will

1. Deepen your understanding of the role of psychosocial functions in mathematics.

2. Learn how to analyze the psychosocial demands of a mathematical task.

3. Deepen your understanding of how to assess a student's strengths and needs in psychosocial functions in math.

4. Broaden your understanding of specific instructional strategies that support psychosocial functions in math.

5. Learn to use your analyses of the neurodevelopmental demands of the task and the strengths and needs of their students to guide planning of adaptations for their math lessons.

WORKSHOP 4   MASTER DESIGN ACTIVITY

1. You and your partner will each need a geoboard and rubber bands and a barrier so that you can't see each other's work.

2. In your team, you will take turns serving in the roles of shape maker and shape guesser. Decide who will be the shape maker and who will be the shape guesser for the first round.

3. With the barrier up between you, the shape maker makes a shape on the geoboard using only one rubber band.

4. The shape maker gives the shape guesser verbal directions for making the shape. Keep the barrier up so that the shape maker can't see how the shape guesser is making the shape. After all directions are given, the shapes are compared.

5. Change roles and do the activity again.

WORKSHOP 4	GROUP SELF-EVALUATION

Name: _____ Date: _____

Task/Problem solved together: _____

How Did It Go?

Circle the numeral that you feel describes your group's actions and behavior.

My group members		Needs Work			Excellent	
1. Listened to one other	1	2	3	4	5
2. Respected all points of view	1	2	3	4	5
3. Concentrated on the work	1	2	3	4	5
4. Shared and worked well	1	2	3	4	5
5. Kept focused on our goal	1	2	3	4	5
6. Were careful not to disturb others	1	2	3	4	5

These are ways our groups can improve:

_____

_____

_____

_____

_____

4.3

WORKSHOP 4 | **WORKSHEET 4A: HANDS-ON EXPLORATION OF THE MATH ACTIVITY**

Watch the video with the teacher's instructions for the activity. Carry out the activity with your group, following the teacher's instructions.

Observe and reflect on what **psychosocial functions** you need to use to carry out this activity. Please use the space below to jot down your observations/reflections:

4.4

Focal Student(s):   *Shamira*

Name of Activity or Lesson Explored: *Symmetry*

Learning Areas (based on Barringer et al., 2010; Levine, 2002; Pohlman, 2008)	What are the demands of the lesson or activity? What roles do these learning areas play in the Symmetry activity?	How does Shamira respond to the demands of the activity? Please note strengths and needs below.	How did the teachers change the Symmetry activity, and what teaching practices do they use to make it more accessible to all students, including Shamira? What additional changes would you make?
Psychosocial *Social Behaviors*			
• **Conflict resolution** (the ability to resolve conflicts with other people without resorting to aggression)			
• **Monitoring** (the ability to watch how you're doing while relating to or interacting with someone)			
• **Self-marketing and image development** (the ability to maintain a good public image and "sell yourself" to others appropriately)			
• **Collaboration** (the ability to cooperate and work with others as a partnership of team effort)			
• **Reading and acting on social information** (the ability to interpret social incidents, people's actions, and gestures and to comprehend concepts such as friendship)			

Social Language

- **Communication and interpretation of feelings**
  (the ability to use and understand word connotations, intonation, and forms of expression so a speaker's true feelings are not distorted)

- **Conversational technique**
  (the ability to engage in a two-way discussion, truly sharing communication)

- **Requesting skills**
  (the ability to know how to ask for something without alienating people)

- **Perspective taking**
  (the ability to assume the perspective of the listener and know how he's feeling while you're speaking)

Higher Thinking
- using and forming concepts
- solving problems
- logical thinking
- creative and critical thinking

Language • understanding mathematical language • using language to communicate with others and to clarify one's ideas			
Spatial Ordering • interpreting relationships within and between spatial patterns • organizing things in space • reasoning with images			
Sequential Ordering • organizing information in sequence • following directions • managing time			
Memory • short-term memory • active working memory • long-term memory			
Attention • controlling mental energy • maintaining focus • self-monitoring			
Motor Coordination • gross motor functions • fine motor functions • grapho-motor functions			

4.7

WORKSHOP 4   **WORKSHEET 4C: LEARNING GOALS**

Your Name: _____ Focal Student Pseudonym: _____

Name of the Lesson: _____

Review the introductory pages for the unit of the *Symmetry* lesson (pages 144 [4.15] to 155 [4.26] and pages 156 [4.27] to 162 [4.33]) to help you answer the questions below.

1. What are the learning goals of the lesson?

2. In what ways do you think this lesson connects to what students have studied in math before (this school year and before)?

3. How do you think what students learn in this lesson will help them with the math they will learn in the future (this school year and beyond)?

WORKSHOP 4	WORKSHEET 4D: TEACHING PRACTICES THAT SUPPORT PSYCHOSOCIAL FUNCTIONS

Think about your focal child (or another child from your classroom). Which of the following teaching practices might work for him or her? How would you use these practices?

Teaching Practices	How would you use these practices with your focal student and other students in your classroom?
Establish a sense of community that is respectful of student differences and conducive to learning.	
Establish norms for working and talking with each other. Review frequently and post in the room.	
Use teacher modeling (act respectful toward all students, reward positive behavior rather than highlight negative behavior).	
Vary group size.	
Establish clear procedures for transitions.	
Use role playing.	
Have students reflect on their group work.	
Scaffold dialog between partners.	
Assign roles.	
Use teacher scaffolding.	

4.9

Cooperative Learning Rules for Group Work

1. You are responsible for your own work and behavior.

2. You must try to answer any question a group member asks.

3. You may only ask a teacher for help when you all have the same question.

4. Every member of the group must be ready to present the group's strategies to the class.

Created by Cindy Wang.

4.10

1. Did your group achieve at least one solution to the problem?

2. Did everybody understand the solution?

3. Did people ask questions when they didn't understand?

4. Was everyone involved in the work?

5. Did the pace of the group work for all the members?

6. Did people give clear explanations?

7. Did everyone have a chance to contribute?

8. Did people listen to one another?

9. Did the group really work well together on the task?

10. Was there enough time for explanation?

Created by Cindy Wang, one of the case lesson teachers.

WORKSHOP 4   **RULES FOR CLASSROOM INTERACTIONS**

Instead of Saying:	Use Respectful Talk
You forgot to say....	I would like to add....
You are wrong....	Here is another way to look at it.
This is not true....	Where did you get your information?
	I see it a different way.
	How would that idea work?

HELP! I HAVE A QUESTION ...

Step 1: Ask myself ...

Step 2: Ask a neighbor.

Step 3: Ask someone at a *nearby* table.

* Ask three people.*

Last: Ask Ms./Mr. [Teacher's Name].

PARTNER TALK:

"What made you think that?"

"Can you show me?"

From Cindy Wang's third-grade classroom.

4.12

WAYS WE SHOW WE ARE GOOD LISTENERS

1. Look at the speaker.

2. Listen quietly to the speaker; ignore distractions.

3. Turn your body toward the speaker.

4. Wait your turn.

5. Nod to show you understand or agree.

6. You can repeat in your own words.

THINGS WE CAN DO TO SOLVE OUR PROBLEMS

1. Walk away. Then, talk it out nicely after some peace time.

2. Do not let it bother you.

3. Give them another chance.

If it still doesn't work ...

4. Respect other people's decisions.

From Cindy Wang's third-grade classroom.

WORKSHOP 4	WORKSHEET 4E: REACTIONS TO THE HANDS-ON EXPLORATION OF THE MATH ACTIVITY

Name: _____

Name of the Lesson: _____

Some things I found interesting when I carried out the activity myself:

1.

2.

3.

Some things I wouldn't have known about the activity if I hadn't explored it hands-on myself:

1.

2.

3.

Unit Guide for the "Symmetry" Lesson

Unit 6 Geometry

overview

In previous grades, *Everyday Mathematics* proceeded from children's experiences with the everyday world to idealized 3-dimensional (3-D) shapes. Children were asked to identify 2-D shapes, edges, and vertices (corners) found within those idealized 3-D shapes. All these experiences led to classifying and naming polygons and circles and to some informal work with angles.

Thus, the progression in previous grades was from 3-D to 2-D. Now, after reviewing 3-D and 2-D figures, the order is reversed. Children start with points and then move on to line segments, rays, and lines. Then they explore the relations among segments, rays, and lines, as well as the geometric figures that can be built from them: angles, polygons, and frames for prisms and pyramids.

contents

UNIT **6**

Unit Organizer **367**

4.16

learning goals in perspective

learning goals	links to the past	links to the future
6a **Developing Goal** Identify, draw, and name line segments, lines, and rays. **(Lessons 6.1 and 6.2)**	Children used straightedges to draw line segments in first grade. In second grade, children defined and named line segments with letter labels. *(Related Grade 3 lessons: 3.2–3.4, 5.6)*	In fourth grade, precision in the use of geometry notation is emphasized. *(Related Grade 3 lessons: 7.9, 8.2, 9.3, 9.10, 9.12, 10.1)*
6b **Developing Goal** Draw parallel and intersecting line segments, lines, and rays. **(Lesson 6.2)**	In first grade, children explored parallel and intersecting line segments through experiences with polygons. The term *parallel* was introduced in second grade. *(Related Grade 3 lessons: 1.4, 3.2–3.4, 5.6)*	Children will continue to construct 2- and 3-dimensional figures to model and explore relationships among parallel and intersecting line segments, lines, and rays. More particular attention to geometry notation will be characteristic of instruction in fourth through sixth grades. *(Related Grade 3 lessons: 7.9, 8.2, 9.3, 9.10, 9.12, 10.1)*
6c **Developing Goal** Draw angles as records of rotations. **(Lesson 6.7)**	Beginning in Kindergarten, children identified and compared angles in plane figures.	In fourth grade, children will continue to work with angles to model turns and rotation. In fifth grade, children will begin to use the Geometry Template and to measure angles in degrees.
6d **Secure Goal** Know multiplication facts from the first set of Fact Triangles. **(Lessons 6.2, 6.6–6.8, and 6.12)**	Multiplication facts were first formally introduced in *Second Grade Everyday Mathematics*. *(Related Grade 3 lessons: 4.5–4.8, 5.1–5.4)*	Throughout third grade, children will practice multiplication facts through games and in a variety of problem-solving situations. Units 7 and 9 also focus on multiplication and division. *(Related Grade 3 lessons: 7.1–7.3, 7.6, 7.8, 9.1–9.6)*
6e **Developing/Secure Goal** Identify right angles. **(Lessons 6.3, 6.7, and 6.8)**	Children informally studied right angles as properties of rectangles and other shapes in earlier grades. *(Related Grade 3 lesson: 3.5)*	In fourth grade, children will continue to work with angles. In fifth grade, children will begin to use the Geometry Template and to measure angles in degrees. *(Related Grade 3 lessons: 7.9, 8.2, 9.3, 9.10)*
6f **Secure Goal** Identify and name 2-D and 3-D shapes. **(Lessons 6.4–6.6, 6.11, and 6.12)**	Children began to examine the properties of 2- and 3-dimensional shapes in Kindergarten. They created models of polygons and polyhedrons in first and second grade. *(Related Grade 3 lessons: 3.5, 3.7, 3.8, 5.6)*	Following third grade, the properties of 2- and 3-dimensional shapes will be reviewed and extended. Terminology and the formal study of area and volume formulas will be emphasized in later grades. *(Related Grade 3 lessons: 7.9, 8.2, 9.3, 9.10, 10.2, 10.3)*
6g **Secure Goal** Identify symmetric figures and draw lines of symmetry. **(Lesson 6.9)**	In Kindergarten and first grade, children began exploring symmetry through art and pattern-block activities and projects. Children made mirror images and found lines of symmetry in second grade.	In fourth grade, children will work with transparent mirrors to investigate reflections and lines of symmetry. They will also explore rotational symmetry and translations.

368 Unit 6 *Geometry*

assessment
—ongoing • product • periodic

☑ Informal Assessment

Math Boxes These *Math Journal* pages provide opportunities for cumulative review or assessment of concepts and skills.

Ongoing Assessment: Kid Watching Use the Ongoing Assessment suggestions in the following lessons to make quick, on-the-spot observations about children's understanding of:
• Numeration **(Lessons 6.1 and 6.10)**
• Operations and Computation **(Lessons 6.2, 6.6, 6.7, and 6.12)**
• Geometry **(Lessons 6.1 and 6.9-6.11)**

Portfolio Ideas Samples of children's work may be obtained from the following assignments:
• Solving a Polygon Cut-up Problem **(Lesson 6.6)**
• Drawing and Decorating a Picture of a Kite **(Lesson 6.9)**
• Creating 8-Point Designs **(Lesson 6.10)**
• Create a Bulletin Board or Book of Pictures with Line Symmetry **(Lesson 6.13)**

☑ Unit 6 Review and Assessment

Math Message Use the question in Lesson 6.13 to assess children's progress toward the following learning goal: Goal 6f

Oral and Slate Assessments Use oral or slate assessments during Lesson 6.13 to assess children's progress toward the following learning goals: Goals 6d, 6e, and 6f

Written Assessment Use a written review during Lesson 6.13 to assess children's progress toward the following learning goals: Goals 6a, 6b, 6c, 6e, 6f, and 6g

Performance/Group Assessment Use a small-group activity in Lesson 6.13 to assess children's progress toward the following learning goals:
Goals 6b, 6c, 6d, and 6g

assessment handbook

For more information on how to use different types of assessment in Unit 6, see the Assessment Overview on pages 58–61 in the *Assessment Handbook*. The following Assessment Masters can be found in the *Math Masters* book:
• Unit 6 Checking Progress, pp. 380 and 381
• Unit 6 Class Checklist, p. 414
• Unit 6 Individual Profile of Progress, p. 415
• Class Progress Indicator, p. 441
• Math Logs, pp. 446–448
• Self-Assessment Forms, pp. 449 and 450
• Interest Inventories, pp. 444 and 445

Unit Organizer **369**

4.18

problemsolving

A process of modeling everyday situations using tools from mathematics

Encourage children to use a variety of strategies when attacking a given problem—and to explain those strategies. *Strategies children might use in this unit:*

- Acting out the problem
- Modeling with manipulatives
- Using estimation
- Making a drawing

Four Problem-Solving REPRESENTATIONS

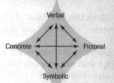

Verbal
Concrete — Pictorial
Symbolic

Lessons that teach *through* problem solving, not just *about* problem solving

Lesson	Activity	Lesson	Activity
6.1	Finding how many line segments can be drawn connecting given points	6.4, 6.5	Estimating the perimeter of a triangle and quadrangle
6.3	Showing angles as turns with connected straws	6.8	Estimating the measures of angles
6.4, 6.5	Doing geometry calisthenics	6.9	Using symmetry to complete designs
6.4, 6.5	Constructing specified triangles and quadrangles with straws and twist-ties	6.10	Finding how many possible shapes can be made with 1 trapezoid and 2 triangle pattern blocks

For more information about problem solving in *Everyday Mathematics*, see the *Teacher's Reference Manual*, pp. 197–208.

cross-curricularlinks

literature

- Discuss *Opt: An Illusionary Tale*, a book that takes place in a kingdom of optical illusions. **(Lesson 6.1)**
- Read *Lao Lao of Dragon Mountain*, a book that explores the Chinese art of paper cutting. **(Lesson 6.9)**

art

- Read the following books about shapes: *The Art of Shapes for Children and Adults* and *Shapes, Shapes, Shapes.* **(Lesson 6.11)**

language arts

- Review the meaning of the prefix *tri-*. **(Lesson 6.4)**
- Review the meaning of the prefix *quad*. **(Lesson 6.5)**
- Discuss the names of polygons and their meanings. **(Lesson 6.6)**

meeting INDIVIDUAL needs
UNIVERSAL ACCESS

◆ RETEACHING

The following features provide additional instructional support:

Adjusting the Activity	Options for Individualizing
• **Lesson 6.2, Part 1**	• **Lesson 6.2** Exploring Line Segments with Geoboards
• **Lesson 6.3, Part 1**	• **Lesson 6.5** Playing *Touch-and-Match Quadrangles*
• **Lesson 6.4, Part 2**	• **Lesson 6.6** Performing Polygon Calisthenics
• **Lesson 6.5, Part 1**	• **Lesson 6.7** Establishing the Need for a Standard Unit of Angle Measure
• **Lesson 6.7, Part 1**	• **Lesson 6.9** Symmetric Kite
• **Lesson 6.8, Part 1**	• **Lesson 6.9** Investigating Symmetry
• **Lesson 6.9, Part 1**	
• **Lesson 6.11, Part 1**	

◆ ENRICHMENT

The following features suggest enrichment and extension activities:

Adjusting the Activity	Options for Individualizing
• **Lesson 6.1, Parts 1, 2**	• **Lesson 6.1** Creating "Curved" Patterns
• **Lesson 6.5, Part 1**	• **Lesson 6.3** Playing the *Robot Game*
• **Lesson 6.8, Part 1**	• **Lesson 6.5** Adding to the Polygon Museum
• **Lesson 6.9, Part 1**	• **Lesson 6.6** Polygons in Literature
• **Lesson 6.10, Part 1**	• **Lesson 6.6** Solving a Polygon Cut-up Problem
• **Lesson 6.12, Part 1**	• **Lesson 6.8** Solving Degree Problems Using a Clock
	• **Lesson 6.9** Line Symmetry in Literature
	• **Lesson 6.11** Constructing a Cube
	• **Lesson 6.12** Modeling a Slanted Cylinder
	• **Lesson 6.12** Examining a Slanted Prism

◆ LANGUAGE DIVERSITY

The following features suggest ways to support children who are acquiring proficiency in English:

Adjusting the Activity	Options for Individualizing
• **Lesson 6.3, Part 1**	• **Lesson 6.1** Making a Vocabulary Chart
• **Lesson 6.7, Part 1**	• **Lessons 6.2–6.5** Adding to the Vocabulary Chart
	• **Lesson 6.10** Shared Reading

◆ MULTIAGE CLASSROOM

The following chart lists related lessons from Grades 2 and 4 that can help you meet your instructional needs:

Grade 2	5.4 5.5	5.4 5.5	5.2 5.3 5.6	4.3 5.1– 5.3	3.4 5.1– 5.6	9.4 9.8	5.2 5.3 5.6	5.2 5.3 5.6	5.9	5.4 5.5 5.9	5.7 5.8	5.7 5.8
Grade 3	6.1	6.2	6.3	6.4	6.5	6.6	6.7	6.8	6.9	6.10	6.11	6.12
Grade 4	1.2	1.2	1.3	1.3	1.3– 1.5	1.5	1.3	1.3		4.1		

materials

lesson	math masters pages	manipulative kit items	other items
6.1	Home Link Master, p. 279 Teaching Masters, pp. 76, 77, 94, and 95	straws and twist-ties	straightedge posterboard *See* **Advance Preparation, p. 378**
6.2	Home Link Master, p. 280	straws and twist-ties geoboard; rubber bands	yardstick or straightedge cords or ropes Vocabulary Chart Fact Triangles
6.3	Home Link Master, p. 281	straws and twist-ties slate (optional)	index cards (optional) Vocabulary Chart
6.4	Home Link Master, p. 282	straws and twist-ties ruler	straightedge loop of rope or cord Vocabulary Chart
6.5	Home Link Master, p. 283 Teaching Master, p. 96	straws and twist-ties ruler	straightedge Vocabulary Chart *See* **Advance Preparation, p. 401**
6.6	Home Link Master, p. 284 Teaching Master, p. 97	straws and twist-ties Pattern-Block Template ruler	straightedge Fact Triangles 20 ft loop of rope or cord *See* **Advance Preparation, p. 407**
6.7	Home Link Master, p. 285 Teaching Master, p. 98	straws and twist-ties meterstick *See* **Advance Preparation, p. 412**	straightedge calculator index card
6.8	Home Link Master, p. 286 Teaching Masters, pp. 99 and 100 transparency of Teaching Master, p. 99 *See* **Advance Preparation, p. 418**	straws and twist-ties 2 six-sided dice	tool-kit clock waxed paper calculator (optional) *Baseball Multiplication* game mat 4 pennies or other counters
6.9	Home Link Master, p. 287 Teaching Masters, pp. 101–104	geoboard; rubber bands pattern blocks ruler	straightedge *See* **Advance Preparation, p. 423**
6.10	Home Link Master, p. 288 Teaching Masters, pp. 105–107	pattern blocks Pattern-Block Template base-10 blocks geoboard; rubber bands	straightedge set of degree-measure cards pennies
6.11	Home Link Master, p. 289 Teaching Masters, pp. 108–111	3-D objects	3-D objects straightedge *See* **Advance Preparation, p. 435**
6.12	Home Link Master, p. 290	4 of each pattern-block shape (per group) number cards	transparent tape Fact Triangles walking-spring toy
6.13	Home Link Masters, pp. 291–294 Assessment Masters, pp. 380 and 381	geoboard; rubber bands	magazines straightedge Fact Triangles *See* **Advance Preparation, p. 446**

372 Unit 6 *Geometry*

4.21

planningtips

Pacing

Pacing depends on a number of factors, such as children's individual needs and how long your school has been using *Everyday Mathematics*. At the beginning of Unit 6, review your Content by Strand Poster to help you set a monthly pace.

← MOST CLASSROOMS →		
J A N U A R Y	F E B R U A R Y	M A R C H

Home Communication

Share Home Links 6.1–6.12 with families to help them understand the content and procedures in this unit. At the end of the unit, use Home Link 6.13 to introduce Unit 7. Supplemental information can be found in the *Home Connection Handbook*.

NCTM Standards

Standard	1	2	3	4	5	6	7	8	9	10
Unit 6 Lessons	1–4, 6–8, 10, 11	2, 3, 10	1–12	4, 7–9	2, 5, 10	1–12	1–12	1–12	1–12	1–12

Content Standards
1 Number and Operations
2 Algebra
3 Geometry
4 Measurement
5 Data Analysis and Probability

Process Standards
6 Problem Solving
7 Reasoning and Proof
8 Communication
9 Connections
10 Representation

PRACTICE *through* Games

Everyday Mathematics uses games to help children develop good fact power and other math skills.

- Compare decimals in *Number Top-It* **(Lesson 6.1)**
- Practice fractions of turns clockwise and counterclockwise in the *Robot Game* **(Lesson 6.3)**
- Name and identify quadrangles in *Touch-and-Match Quadrangles* **(Lesson 6.5)**
- Practice multiplication facts in *Beat the Calculator* **(Lesson 6.7)**
- Practice multiplication facts with *Baseball Multiplication* **(Lesson 6.8)**
- Practice with angle measures in *Angle Race* **(Lessons 6.9 and 6.10)**

unit 6 content highlights

The notes below highlight the major content ideas presented in Unit 6. These notes may help you establish instructional priorities.

The Vocabulary of Geometry

The primary emphasis in Unit 6 is on developing an intuitive grasp of relations among and classifications of geometric figures, not on memorizing vocabulary. This does not mean that you should shy away from *using* the vocabulary of geometry. Children will not be familiar with all the terms that come up in this unit, but keep in mind that with repeated use, these words will become part of their vocabularies.

Nor will children always use geometric terms correctly. That's fine. If you use words consistently, children will gradually develop the working vocabulary essential for discussing the characteristics of figures, as well as the similarities and differences among them. Whenever you have the opportunity, take the time to discuss the derivations, roots, prefixes, and suffixes of geometric terms. For example, the word *polygon* comes from the Greek words *poly-,* which means *many,* and *gonia,* which means *angle.* Terms for other polygons build on this; thus, *pentagon* means five angles, and *hexagon* means six angles. *Triangle* means three angles, and *quadrangle* means four angles. In *Third Grade Everyday Mathematics,* the term *quadrangle* is used instead of *quadrilateral,* so that all polygons are named in terms of the number of angles.

Three-Dimensional Shapes (Lessons 6.11 and 6.12)

Using objects from the Shapes Museum and diagrams in the *Student Reference Book,* children review similarities and differences among five kinds of 3-D shapes (prisms, pyramids, spheres, cylinders, and cones) and the five regular polyhedrons.

NOTE: The concepts of faces and bases of prisms and pyramids can cause confusion. *All* the surfaces of prisms and pyramids are faces; but bases are *special* faces.

▷ The bases of a prism come in pairs that are opposite *and* parallel to each other. They can be any polygon shape.

▷ Prisms are named after the shapes of their bases, such as *triangular* prism and *rectangular* prism. The other faces of a prism must be either rectangular or in the shape of a nonrectangular parallelogram. In a rectangular prism or cube, any opposite faces can be bases.

▷ A pyramid has only one base. The other faces are triangular and come together in a point. As with prisms, pyramids are named after the shapes of their bases. In a triangular pyramid, *any* face can be a base.

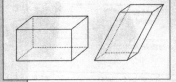

Rectangular prism and slanted prism

▷ A cylinder is like a prism in that it has a pair of bases. A cone is like a pyramid in that it has only one base. Cylinders and cones differ from prisms and pyramids in that they have curved surfaces.

▷ Spheres have no faces; they are completely curved.

A polyhedron (from the Greek, *poly-*, meaning *many*, and *hedra*, meaning *face*) is a 3-D shape whose faces are all formed by polygons. A regular polyhedron is a polyhedron whose faces are all identical (congruent). People have known for thousands of years that there are only five regular polyhedrons. One of them—the tetrahedron—is a triangular pyramid; another—the cube—is a square prism. The other three, which are neither prisms nor pyramids, are the octahedron (8 faces), dodecahedron (12 faces), and icosahedron (20 faces).

Two-dimensional figures are abstractions within a plane and have no thickness, while 3-dimensional figures in some sense project out of a plane. In the real world, of course, any representation of a 2-D figure is really 3-dimensional—even pencil marks have some thickness. This is also true of shapes made out of straws, pattern blocks, or rubber bands on geoboards. Children may find an occasional discussion of this fact interesting, but are perfectly willing to take such representations as "almost" 2-dimensional.

Points, Segments, Rays, and Lines (Lessons 6.1 and 6.2)

Points, line segments, rays, and lines are geometric abstractions. For example, a point is an exact location in space and, as such, has no size. Dots, which do have size, are not really points; they are used to represent points. Points are usually named with capital letters.

A line segment is a set of points that traces the shortest path between two points. When we draw a "straight line" connecting two points, the drawing is a representation of a line segment, not the line segment itself.

Similarly, rays and lines exist only in our imaginations, especially since they extend endlessly in one or two directions. As with number lines, arrows represent these infinite extensions when rays and lines are represented. These figures can be named by naming points on them.

Pairs of lines in the same plane either intersect, or meet, at one point, or they never meet, in which case they are said to be parallel. As with lines, intersecting segments or rays also meet at one point. Segments and rays are said to be parallel if they can be extended into parallel lines. Parallel lines, segments, and rays are everywhere the same distance apart.

Straw with twist-tie arrowheads

In Unit 6, these relations between and among lines, segments, and rays are explored by performing geometry "calisthenics," by making straw constructions, by observing shapes in the Shapes Museum, or simply by exercising one's imagination.

Unit Organizer **375**

4.24

parallelogram

rectangle

square

rhombus

trapezoid

kite

NOTE: This information is presented here to provide some background. These ideas are abstract and need not be discussed at this stage in children's development. They will be brought up in later grades.

Forming Figures from Rays and Segments (Lessons 6.3–6.6)

Angles are often described as two rays or two line segments that originate at the same endpoint. Unit 6 emphasizes a more dynamic approach: *Angles can be represented by rotating one ray while the other side is kept stationary.* The amount of rotation serves as an intuitive introduction to angle measure. To help children visualize the differences in sizes of angles, have them each extend one arm. Then, ask them to think of the upper and lower parts of their arms as two sides of an angle and of their elbows as the vertices. Show them how to trace the arc of the angle formed between their upper and lower arms with their other hands. As they pull their lower arms inward, the angle becomes smaller; as they extend their lower arms outward, the angle becomes larger until it becomes straight—a line segment.

The stationary-turn and other geometry calisthenics are similar to "playing turtle" with a computer program. You can also compare stationary-turn calisthenics to group drills with bands, drill teams, or military drill practice. An "about face" would be a request to make a half-turn; "right face" would be a quarter-turn to the right (or clockwise); and "left face" would be a quarter-turn to the left (or counterclockwise). You can also ask children to make equivalent turns. For example, a "quarter-turn left" is equivalent to a "three-quarters turn right." Turn-and-move "calisthenics" can be further extended via the *Robot Game*, in which a "Controller" gives directions for turns and steps until the "Robot" reaches a destination.

Polygons are 2-dimensional figures made up of line segments. When representing a polygon, one may draw a path starting at one point and returning to that point, without the path crossing over itself. A polygon is a boundary; the region inside the polygon is *not* part of the polygon. Pairs of sides of a polygon meet at a point called a vertex. The vertices of a polygon can be used to name the polygon.

Children review these ideas through calisthenics, drawings with a straightedge, and straw constructions; they also classify triangles, quadrangles, and other polygons.

You will need to pay special attention to the classification for quadrangles—any four-sided polygons. Parallelograms are special kinds of quadrangles: Both pairs of opposite sides are parallel and equal in size. Parallelograms include rectangles, all of whose angles are right angles; squares, all of whose sides and angles are the same size; and rhombuses, all of whose sides are the same length. Thus, squares, rectangles, and rhombuses are all parallelograms, and squares are also rectangles. Trapezoids and kites are quadrangles, but not parallelograms. Trapezoids have only one pair of opposite parallel sides. Kites have no parallel sides, but they do have two pairs of adjacent sides (sides with a vertex in common) that are the same length.

These definitions can be very confusing, and not all people agree on the details. Try to use these terms as correctly as possible. Children are familiar with some of them from their experiences with the actual shapes, and they will pick up the precise definitions over time.

Line Symmetry (Lesson 6.9)

Symmetric shapes can be divided by a line into two halves that are exact "mirror images" of each other. Shapes with approximate symmetry abound in the everyday world—people, buildings, designs, furniture, and so on. Children explore symmetry through paper folding, drawing, and geoboard activities. They see that a shape can have more than one line of symmetry.

Review and Assessment (Lesson 6.13)

This unit continues to explore various geometric figures, relationships between and among these figures, and ways to classify them. One of the best ways to assess children's understanding of geometry concepts is through ongoing observations and questions as children participate in various activities and discussions. Although children may not be able to put formal definitions into words, they can describe a concept informally, point out an example, and correctly use terms in context.

Lesson 6.13 assesses children's ability to identify, name, and draw various 2-D and 3-D shapes, draw angles as records of rotations, and identify symmetric figures.

If you are planning a quarterly assessment for Units 3–6, you may want to refer to the *Assessment Handbook*. The quarterly learning goals Class Checklist, and Individual Profile of Progress checklist (*Math Masters*, pages 429–431) are useful tools for keeping track of children's progress.

Real butterflies are approximately symmetric.

Man-made figures can be drawn to be symmetric.

For additional information on the following topics, see the *Teacher's Reference Manual*:

- angles and rotations
- dimension
- geometry
- lines, segments, and rays
- parallel and perpendicular
- points
- polygons
- solid figures
- symmetry
- teaching geometry

Unit Organizer   **377**

6.9 Symmetry

OBJECTIVES To review the meaning of symmetry; and to explore properties of symmetric shapes.

summaries   materials

1   Teaching the Lesson

summaries	materials
Children fold and cut out a symmetric figure; explore the properties of symmetric figures; connect matching points on mirror images; and draw the missing halves of symmetric shapes. [Geometry]	☐ *Math Journal 1*, p. 147 ☐ Home Link 6.8 ☐ *Student Reference Book* ☐ Teaching Master (*Math Masters*, p. 101) ☐ scissors; straightedge; hand mirror (optional) ☐ cm ruler *See* **Advance Preparation**

2   Ongoing Learning & Practice

summaries	materials
Children play *Angle Race*. [Geometry] Children practice and maintain skills through Math Boxes and Home Link activities.	☐ *Math Journal 1*, p. 148 ☐ *Student Reference Book* ☐ Teaching Master (*Math Masters*, p. 102) ☐ Home Link Master (*Math Masters*, p. 287) ☐ 24-pin circular geoboard and rubber bands, or circular geoboard paper (*Math Masters*, p. 103) ☐ straightedge *See* **Advance Preparation**

3   Options for Individualizing

summaries	materials
Enrichment The teacher or children read *Lao Lao of Dragon Mountain*. [Geometry] **Reteaching** Children draw a design on half of a kite and then draw its mirror image. [Geometry] **Reteaching** Children explore symmetry with geoboards or pattern blocks. [Geometry]	☐ Teaching Master (*Math Masters*, p. 104) ☐ markers or colored pencils ☐ geoboard and rubber bands ☐ pattern blocks ☐ *Lao Lao of Dragon Mountain* *See* **Advance Preparation**

Additional Information

Advance Preparation Obtain a hand mirror for an activity in Part 1 (optional).

Copy and cut out *Angle Race* degree-measure cards from *Math Masters*, page 102.

For the optional Enrichment activity in Part 3, obtain the book *Lao Lao of Dragon Mountain* by Margaret Bateson-Hill (De Agostini Children's Books, 1996).

Vocabulary • symmetric • symmetry • mirror image • line of symmetry

| WORKSHOP 4 | LESSON GUIDE FOR THE "SYMMETRY" LESSON |

Getting Started

Mental Math and Reflexes

Pose equal-sharing and equal-grouping division number stories. *Suggestions:*

- 4 children share 14 envelopes equally. How many envelopes does each child get? 3 How many envelopes are left over? 2
- 24 muffins are packed 6 to a package. How many packages are there? 4 How many leftover muffins? 0

Math Message

Take a copy of Math Masters, *page 101. Use a straightedge to draw line segments to connect the dots in order: A to B, B to C, and so on. Fold the shape carefully along the dotted line so that the dotted and solid lines are on the outside. Keep it folded. Cut along the solid lines. Unfold the cutout piece.*

Home Link 6.8 Follow-Up

Briefly go over the answers. Make sure children understand that the arc shows the path and the direction of the rotation.

1 Teaching the Lesson

◆ Math Message Follow-Up (*Math Masters*, p. 101)

 WHOLE-CLASS ACTIVITY

Ask children what kind of figure the cutout piece is. A kite Ask them to explain why the kite is **symmetric,** or has **symmetry.** When the shape is folded, the two halves match.

> **Adjusting the Activity** Provide a variety of magazines for children to look through and from which they can cut out pictures of objects that have symmetry.

◆ Exploring Properties of Symmetric Figures (*Math Masters*, p. 101)

WHOLE-CLASS ACTIVITY

Ask the children to fold their cutout kites. Show them how to punch a hole with a pencil point or hole-puncher through both halves at each of the labeled points, except *A* and *J*. Children then use a straightedge to connect the holes on the blank half of the kite in the same pattern as on the other half of the kite.

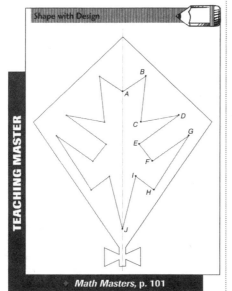

TEACHING MASTER

Shape with Design

◆ *Math Masters*, p. 101

424 Unit 6 *Geometry*

4.28

WORKSHOP 4   **LESSON GUIDE FOR THE "SYMMETRY" LESSON**

When they unfold their kites, children will notice that they have drawn a pattern that looks very much like the existing pattern. If you have a hand mirror, place it straight up on the fold line. Ask someone to describe what he or she sees in the mirror. The pattern children have drawn is called the **mirror image** of the existing pattern. Discuss the relationship between the existing pattern and its mirror image. Ask: *How are they alike?* They are the same size and have the same shape. *How are they different?* They face in opposite directions.

Have children use a straightedge to connect a pair of matching points—a point on the right side to its corresponding point on the left side. Repeat for two other pairs of matching points.

For each pair of matching points, have children measure the distance in centimeters from each point to the fold line. Ask what they observe. The distance from one point to the fold line is the same as the distance from its matching point to the fold line. Some children may mention that the line segments connecting pairs of matching points form right angles with the fold line.

After children have finished connecting pairs of matching points and measuring the distance from each point to the fold line, discuss the following concepts:

▷ A shape is *symmetric* if it can be folded in half so that the two halves match.

▷ The fold line is called the **line of symmetry.**

▷ The *mirror image* of a design is the same size and shape as the design, but it faces in the opposite direction.

✦ Completing Symmetric Figures
(*Math Journal 1*, p. 147; *Student Reference Book*, pp. 111 and 112)

PARTNER ACTIVITY

Partners draw the missing halves of symmetric figures. Ask children to describe how they solved Exercise 9.

Children can read more about line symmetry on pages 111 and 112 of the *Student Reference Book.*

☑ **ONGOING ASSESSMENT**
Children are expected to understand the concept of line symmetry. Use journal page 147 to assess their skill levels.

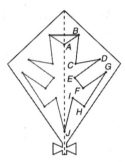

B's matching point connected

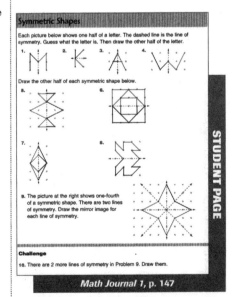

Math Journal 1, p. 147

STUDENT PAGE

Lesson 6.9   **425**

WORKSHOP 4   **LESSON GUIDE FOR THE "SYMMETRY" LESSON**

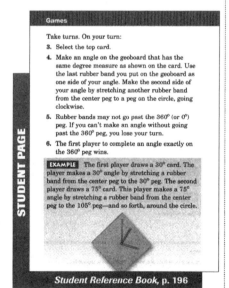

STUDENT PAGE

Games

Angle Race

Materials
☐ 24-pin circular geoboard, or Circular Geoboard Paper (*Math Masters*, p. 103)
☐ rubber bands, or straightedge and pencil
☐ set of degree-measure cards (*Math Masters*, p. 102)

Players   2

Directions

1. Shuffle the cards. Place them facedown.

2. If you have a circular geoboard, stretch a rubber band from the center peg to the 0° peg. If you do *not* have a circular geoboard, use circular geoboard paper. Draw a line segment from the center dot to the 0° dot. Instead of stretching rubber bands, you will draw line segments.

Student Reference Book, p. 195

 Ongoing Learning & Practice

◆ Playing *Angle Race*
(*Math Masters*, pp. 102 and 103;
Student Reference Book, pp. 195 and 196)

PARTNER ACTIVITY

Children practice measurement skills by playing *Angle Race*. For detailed instructions, work through the directions on *Student Reference Book*, pages 195 and 196 with the children.

◆ Math Boxes 6.9 (*Math Journal 1*, p. 148)

INDEPENDENT ACTIVITY

Mixed Review This journal page provides opportunities for cumulative review or assessment of concepts and skills.

◆ Home Link 6.9 (*Math Masters*, p. 287)

Home Connection Children fold sheets of paper to create lines of symmetry and answer questions about the shapes that they create.

STUDENT PAGE

Games

Take turns. On your turn:

3. Select the top card.

4. Make an angle on the geoboard that has the same degree measure as shown on the card. Use the last rubber band you put on the geoboard as one side of your angle. Make the second side of your angle by stretching another rubber band from the center peg to a peg on the circle, going clockwise.

5. Rubber bands may not go past the 360° (or 0°) peg. If you can't make an angle without going past the 360° peg, you lose your turn.

6. The first player to complete an angle exactly on the 360° peg wins.

EXAMPLE The first player draws a 30° card. The player makes a 30° angle by stretching a rubber band from the center peg to the 30° peg. The second player draws a 75° card. This player makes a 75° angle by stretching a rubber band from the center peg to the 105° peg—and so forth, around the circle.

Student Reference Book, p. 196

426   **Unit 6** *Geometry*

TEACHING MASTER

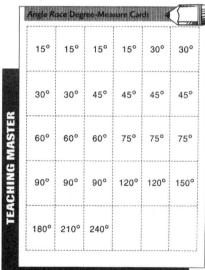

Angle Race Degree-Measure Cards

15°	15°	15°	15°	30°	30°
30°	30°	45°	45°	45°	45°
60°	60°	60°	75°	75°	75°
90°	90°	90°	120°	120°	150°
180°	210°	240°			

Math Masters, p. 102

Options for Individualizing

◆ ENRICHMENT Line Symmetry in Literature

WHOLE-CLASS ACTIVITY   **5–15 min**

Literature Link *Lao Lao of Dragon Mountain* by Margaret Bateson-Hill (De Agostini Children's Books, 1996) tells the story of a woman who makes beautiful paper cutouts for children in her village. A greedy emperor has her imprisoned in a tower and demands that she make a chest full of jewels for him. Patterns for cutting some of the symmetric shapes shown in the book are included so that children can explore the Chinese art of paper cutting.

◆ RETEACHING Symmetric Kite
(*Math Masters*, p. 104)

INDEPENDENT ACTIVITY   **5–15 min**

Children draw a design on one half of the kite on *Math Masters*, page 104. Then they draw its mirror image on the other half and color the kite. You may want to use children's work for a bulletin-board display.

Portfolio Ideas

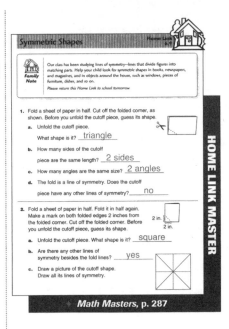

Symmetric Shapes   Home Link

Family Note Our class has been studying lines of symmetry—lines that divide figures into matching parts. Help your child look for symmetric shapes in books, newspapers, and magazines, and in objects around the house, such as windows, pieces of furniture, dishes, and so on.
Please return this Home Link to school tomorrow.

1. Fold a sheet of paper in half. Cut off the folded corner, as shown. Before you unfold the cutoff piece, guess its shape.
   a. Unfold the cutoff piece.
      What shape is it? __triangle__
   b. How many sides of the cutoff piece are the same length? __2 sides__
   c. How many angles are the same size? __2 angles__
   d. The fold is a line of symmetry. Does the cutoff piece have any other lines of symmetry? __no__

2. Fold a sheet of paper in half. Fold it in half again. Make a mark on both folded edges 2 inches from the folded corner. Cut off the folded corner. Before you unfold the cutoff piece, guess its shape.
   a. Unfold the cutoff piece. What shape is it? __square__
   b. Are there any other lines of symmetry besides the fold lines? __yes__
   c. Draw a picture of the cutoff shape. Draw all its lines of symmetry.

◆ *Math Masters, p. 287*

 Math Boxes 6.9

1. Draw a line segment, $\overline{DI}$, parallel to the line, $\overline{PO}$. Draw a ray, $\overline{LA}$, that intersects the line, $\overline{TW}$.
   Sample answer:

2. Describe a regular polygon.
   Sample answer:
   A regular polygon is a polygon whose sides all have the same length, and whose angles are all the same size.

3. Fill in the unit box. Then multiply.
   $4 \times 5 = $ __20__
   $7 \times 3 = $ __21__
   __16__ $= 4 \times 4$
   __15__ $= 5 \times 3$
   __35__ $= 7 \times 5$

4. The degree measure of the angle is
   ○ more than 90°.
   ● less than 90°.
   ○ more than 180°.
   ○ 120°.

5. Measure each side of the quadrangle to the nearest half-centimeter.
   $2\frac{1}{2}$ cm $2\frac{1}{2}$ cm $2\frac{1}{2}$ cm
   5 cm
   Another name for this quadrangle is __trapezoid__

6. Circle the right angle.

◆ *Math Journal 1, p. 148*

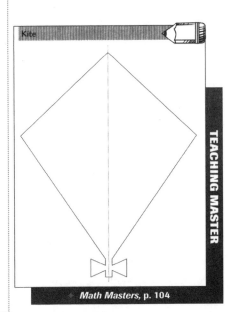

Kite

◆ *Math Masters, p. 104*

◆ **RETEACHING** **Investigating Symmetry**

SMALL-GROUP ACTIVITY   **5–15 min**

If children are struggling with the concept of symmetry, consider the following activities:

1. Have children work with geoboards. First, divide the geoboard in half with a rubber band.

Divided geoboard

Then use another rubber band to create a simple shape on the right-hand side.

One-half of a symmetric design

Ask a child to create the other half of the shape with a third rubbber band.

The child completes the design.

2. Use pattern blocks to create designs. First, fold a blank sheet of paper in half widthwise to create a line of symmetry. Then unfold the paper and lay it flat on the table.

Next, make a simple design with pattern blocks on the right side of the paper.

Then ask a child to create the other half of the design.

Paper provides the background for a symmetric design.

One-half of a design

The child completes the design.

428   **Unit 6** *Geometry*

4.32

From *Everyday Mathematics, Grade 3, Volume 1*. Copyright by The McGraw-Hill Companies. Used by permission. All rights reserved.

WORKSHOP 4 | **GEOMETRIC SHAPES**

4.34

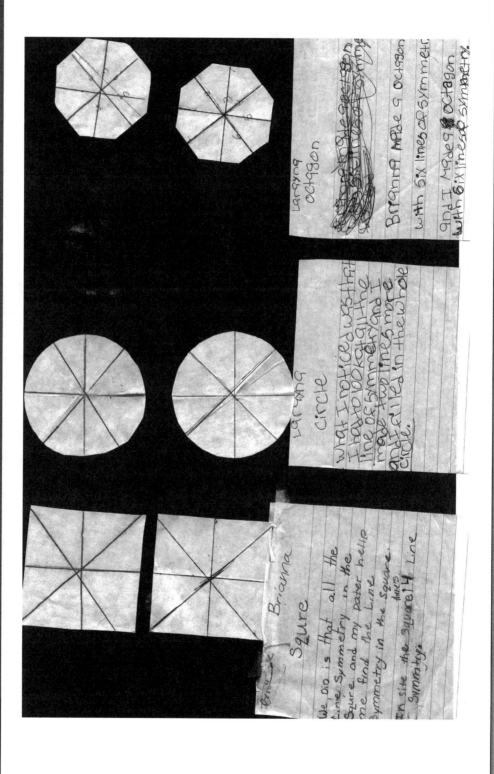

4.37

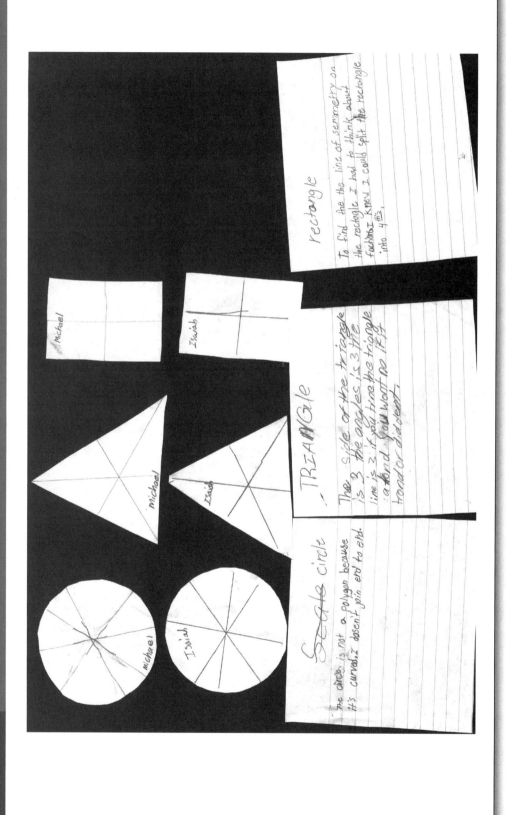

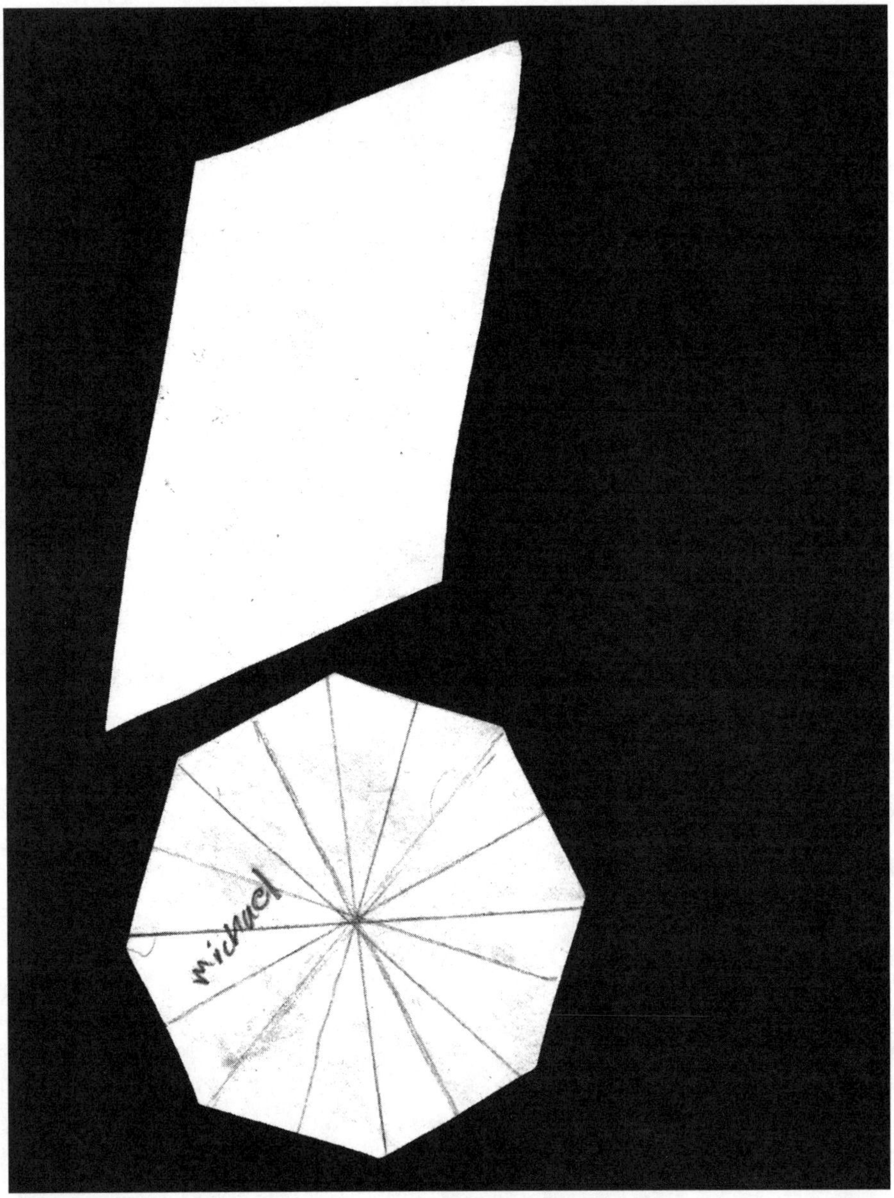
michael

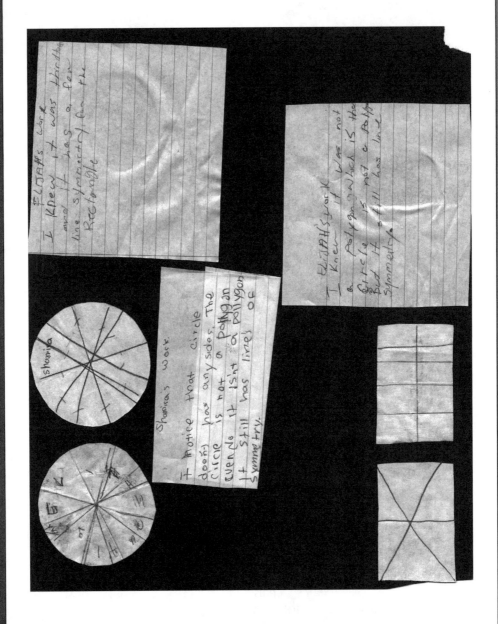

WORKSHOP 4   HOMEWORK ASSIGNMENT

In preparation for our next Math for All Workshop, please complete the following assignments:

1. Plan and implement a math lesson that supports students' psychosocial functions.

   - Select a lesson that you will teach before our next workshop. Consult with the colleagues in your team. Read the description of the lesson and enact it with your colleagues (actually do the work of the lesson; don't just think about how it will be done). Analyze the goals and the psychosocial demands of the lesson. Take notes in the second column of the Lesson Planning Chart. Also complete Worksheet 4E (Reactions to the Hands-on Exploration of the Math Activity).
   - Think about the strengths and needs of your focal child(ren), and take some notes about how you expect the child or the children to respond to the psychosocial demands of the task. Add your notes in the third column of the Lesson Planning Chart (if you need more space, use extra copies of the chart).
   - Together with the colleagues in your team, plan some adaptations for the lesson that address the psychosocial strengths and needs of the focal child(ren). Record your ideas in the fourth column of the Lesson Planning Chart.
   - Implement the lesson with the adaptations. If possible, invite the members of your team to observe the lesson. (You may want to videotape the focal child so that you and your colleagues can examine him or her as a team.) Have one or more members of your team observe your focal child(ren). Record your observations on the Observation Chart.
   - Answer the lesson analysis questions.

Make sure to bring the completed Learning Goals Worksheet, Lesson Planning Chart, and Observation Chart as well as your answers to the Lesson Analysis Questions to the next workshop session. Your group may be asked to share your observations, as well as and the facilitators will collect your charts and reflections so they can learn more about the children in your classrooms and your thinking about them. Feel free to submit the Lesson Goals worksheet and Lesson Planning and Observation Charts as a group. However, please answer the Lesson Analysis Questions individually.

2. Please read one of the following chapters:

   - Chapter 9 ("Our Social Thinking System") from *A Mind at a Time*.
   - Chapter 11, pp. 214–216 ("Social Cognition") from *Revealing Minds*.

3. Bring curriculum guides and materials for lesson planning.

   You will need to use these materials during the workshop to do some planning for a lesson that you will teach after the fifth workshop session. The focus of this planning will be on higher order thinking. Together with your team, please think of a lesson you might want to focus on. Make sure to bring the curriculum guide for that lesson, and if possible, the manipulatives that go with that lesson to our next workshop.

Your Name: _____

Focal Student Pseudonym: _____

Name of the Lesson: _____

Review the introductory pages for the lesson (and its unit) you are planning to help you answer the questions below.

1. What are the learning goals of the lesson?

2. In what ways do you think this lesson connects to what students have studied in math before (this school year and before)?

3. How do you think what students learn in this lesson will help them with the math they will learn in the future (this school year and beyond)?

4.43

WORKSHOP 4 **WORKSHEET 4G: HANDS-ON EXPLORATION OF THE MATH ACTIVITY**

Read the description of the lesson and enact it with your colleagues. It is important to actually carry out the focal activity of the lesson. Don't just think about how it will be done.

Observe and reflect on what **psychosocial functions** you need to use to carry out this activity. Please use the space below to jot down your observations/reflections:

4.44

Your Name: _____

Name of Activity or Lesson Explored: _____   Focal Student Pseudonym: _____

Learning Areas (based on Barringer et al., 2010; Levine, 2002; Pohlman, 2008)	What are the demands of the lesson or activity? What roles do these learning areas play in the Symmetry activity?	How does Shamira respond to the demands of the activity? Please note strengths and needs below.	How did the teachers change the Symmetry activity, and what teaching practices do they use to make it more accessible to all students, including Shamira? What additional changes would you make?
Psychosocial *Social Behaviors* • **Conflict resolution** (the ability to resolve conflicts with other people without resorting to aggression)			
• **Monitoring** (the ability to watch how you're doing while relating to or interacting with someone)			
• **Self-marketing and image development** (the ability to maintain a good public image and "sell yourself" to others appropriately)			
• **Collaboration** (the ability to cooperate and work with others as a partnership of team effort)			

• **Reading and acting on social information** (the ability to interpret social incidents, people's actions, and gestures and to comprehend concepts such as friendship)					
Social Language • **Communication and interpretation of feelings** (the ability to use and understand word connotations, intonation, and forms of expression so a speaker's true feelings are not distorted)					
• **Conversational technique** (the ability to engage in a two-way discussion, truly sharing communication)					
• **Requesting skills** (the ability to know how to ask for something without alienating people)					
• **Perspective taking** (the ability to assume the perspective of the listener and know how he or she is feeling while you're speaking)					
Higher Thinking • using and forming concepts • solving problems • logical thinking • creative and critical thinking					

Language • understanding mathematical language • using language to communicate with others and to clarify one's ideas					
Spatial Ordering • interpreting relationships within and between spatial patterns • organizing things in space • reasoning with images					
Sequential Ordering • organizing information in sequence • following directions • managing time					
Memory • short-term memory • active working memory • long-term memory					
Attention • controlling mental energy • maintaining focus • self-monitoring					
Motor Coordination • gross motor functions • fine motor functions • grapho-motor functions					

Psychosocial Functions

Your Name: _____

Name of Activity or Lesson Explored: _____

Focal Student Pseudonym: _____

Learning Areas (based on Barringer et al., 2010; Levine, 2002; Pohlman, 2008)	How did the focal student handle the various demands of the activity or lesson? Note your observations below.
Psychosocial	
Social Behaviors	
• **Conflict resolution** (the ability to resolve conflicts with other people without resorting to aggression)	
• **Monitoring** (the ability to watch how you're doing while relating to or interacting with someone)	
• **Self-marketing and image development** (the ability to maintain a good public image and "sell yourself" to others appropriately)	
• **Collaboration** (the ability to cooperate and work with others as a partnership of team effort)	

• **Reading and acting on social information** (the ability to interpret social incidents, people's actions, and gestures and to comprehend concepts such as friendship)					
Social Language • **Communication and interpretation of feelings** (the ability to use and understand word connotations, intonation, and forms of expression so a speaker's true feelings are not distorted)					
• **Conversational technique** (the ability to engage in a two-way discussion, truly sharing communication)					
• **Requesting skills** (the ability to know how to ask for something without alienating people)					
• **Perspective taking** (the ability to assume the perspective of the listener and know how he's feeling while you're speaking)					
Higher Thinking • using and forming concepts • solving problems • logical thinking • creative and critical thinking					

Language • understanding mathematical language • using language to communicate with others and to clarify one's ideas	
Spatial Ordering • interpreting relationships within and between spatial patterns • organizing things in space • reasoning with images	
Sequential Ordering • organizing information in sequence • following directions • managing time	
Memory • short-term memory • active working memory • long-term memory	
Attention • controlling mental energy • maintaining focus • self-monitoring	
Motor Coordination • gross motor functions • fine motor functions • grapho-motor functions	

WORKSHOP 4 | **LESSON ANALYSIS QUESTIONS**

Your Name: _____ Focal Student Pseudonym: _____

1. What changes did you and your team make to the original lesson?

2. What do you think students learned? Did they reach the goal(s) of the lesson?

3. Did the students do what you expected them to do? Were there any surprises?

4. Were there any students who didn't participate fully?

5. Did your focal student work as you had hoped he or she would?

6. In what ways did the changes you and your team made to the lesson help the focal student? Did these changes help other students as well?

7. If you were to teach or assist with this lesson again, what would you do differently?

8. How has this assignment influenced your work with students (or teachers)?

Workshop 5

Supporting Higher Order Thinking Functions

This workshop focuses on higher order thinking. You will consider the role of higher order thinking in learning math, and learn about how the neurodevelopmental framework describes various components of higher order thinking. The case lesson for this workshop is a fifth-grade lesson on multiplication. You will examine the higher order thinking demands of the focal activity, which requires students to solve a multiplication cluster problem. You will observe Michael to assess his strengths and needs in higher order thinking. You will also watch video clips of the teacher to identify and discuss specific strategies for supporting higher order thinking in this lesson.

Using the same process as in previous workshops, you will work in teams to plan higher order thinking adaptations for a lesson that you will teach in the near future.

You will

1. Deepen your understanding of the role of higher order thinking in mathematics.

2. Learn how to analyze the higher order thinking demands of a mathematical task.

3. Deepen your understanding of how to assess a student's strengths and needs in higher order thinking in math.

4. Broaden your understanding of specific instructional strategies that support higher order thinking in math.

5. Learn to use your analyses of the neurodevelopmental demands of the task and the strengths and needs of their students to guide planning of adaptations for their math lessons.

Divide Each Shape Into Four Congruent Parts

WORKSHOP 5	ADAPTED WORKSHEET FOR "MULTIPLICATION CLUSTER PROBLEMS" LESSON

Your Name: _____ Date: _____

Writing About Multiplication Clusters

Solve this cluster of problems and write about how you solved it. Tell how you used one answer to help you find another answer.

10 × 21	2 × 21
5 × 21	50 × 21
52 × 21	

The number sentence that helped me solve the final problem was

_____

This was helpful because

_____

_____

_____

A MUTLPLICATION SITAUTION   _____ × _____

With the other members of your math team, choose one of the number sentences to write a multiplication story. Write it on your chart paper and then record it in the space below.

Problem:

_____

_____

_____

Solution:

_____
| |
_____

1	2	3	4	5	6	7	8	9	10
11	12	13	14	15	16	17	18	19	20
21	22	23	24	25	26	27	28	29	30
31	32	33	34	35	36	37	38	39	40
41	42	43	44	45	46	47	48	49	50
51	52	53	54	55	56	57	58	59	60
61	62	63	64	65	66	67	68	69	70
71	72	73	74	75	76	77	78	79	80
81	82	83	84	85	86	87	88	89	90
91	92	93	94	95	96	97	98	99	100
101	102	103	104	105	106	107	108	109	110
111	112	113	114	115	116	117	118	119	120
121	122	123	124	125	126	127	128	129	130
131	132	133	134	135	136	137	138	139	140
141	142	143	144	145	146	147	148	149	150
151	152	153	154	155	156	157	158	159	160
161	162	163	164	165	166	167	168	169	170
171	172	173	174	175	176	177	178	179	180
181	182	183	184	185	186	187	188	189	190
191	192	193	194	195	196	197	198	199	200
201	202	203	204	205	206	207	208	209	210
211	212	213	214	215	216	217	218	219	220
221	222	223	224	225	226	227	228	229	230
231	232	233	234	235	236	237	238	239	240
241	242	243	244	245	246	247	248	249	250
251	252	253	254	255	256	257	258	259	260
261	262	263	264	265	266	267	268	269	270
271	272	273	274	275	276	277	278	279	280
281	282	283	284	285	286	287	288	289	290
291	292	293	294	295	296	297	298	299	300

5.4

WORKSHOP 5	WORKSHEET 5A: HANDS-ON EXPLORATION OF THE MATH ACTIVITY

Watch the video with the teacher's instructions for the activity. Carry out the activity with your group, following the teacher's instructions.

Observe and reflect on what **higher order thinking** you need to use to carry out this activity. Please use the space below to jot down your observations/reflections:

Focal Student: *Michael*

Name of Activity or Lesson Explored: *Multiplication Cluster Problems*

Learning Areas (based on Barringer et al., 2010; Levine, 2002; Pohlman, 2008)	What are the demands of the *Multiplication Cluster Problems* activity? What roles do these learning areas play in the lesson activity?	How does Michael respond to the demands of the activity? Please note strengths and needs below.	How did Vilma Caban change the *Multiplication Cluster* activity, and what teaching practices does she use to make it more accessible to all students, including Michael? What additional changes would you make?
Higher Order Thinking			
• **Thinking with concepts** (a concept may be abstract, concrete, a process, verbal, or nonverbal)			
• **Problem solving** (involves knowing it's a problem, previewing outcomes, assessing feasibility, mobilizing resources, logical thinking, strategies, starting and pacing, self-monitoring, dealing with impasses, and reflecting)			
• **Critical thinking** (involves knowing the facts, the creator's point of view, your point of view, errors and exaggerations and getting outside help, weighing the evidence, communicating)			
• **Rule-guided thinking** (if...then kinds of thinking)			
• **Creative thinking** (involves divergent thinking, taking a fresh look, suspension of self-evaluation, and risk taking)			

5.6

Category		
Language • understanding mathematical language • using language to communicate with others and to clarify one's ideas		
Spatial Ordering • interpreting relationships within and between spatial patterns • organizing things in space • reasoning with images		
Sequential Ordering • organizing information in sequence • following directions • managing time		
Memory • short-term memory • active working memory • long-term memory		
Attention • controlling mental energy • maintaining focus • self-monitoring		
Psychosocial • using and understanding social language • collaboration • conflict resolution		
Motor Coordination • gross motor functions • fine motor functions • grapho-motor functions		

5.7

WORKSHOP 5	WORKSHEET 5C: LEARNING GOALS

Your Name:_____ Focal Student Pseudonym: _____

Name of the Lesson: _____

Review the description of the "Multiplication Cluster Problem" lesson to help you answer the questions below. You can find the unit overview on pages 191 (5.10) to 201 (5.20), the lesson guide on pages 202 (5.21) to 209 (5.28), and the original student worksheets on pages 210 (5.29) to 212 (5.31) of your participant booklet.

1. What are the learning goals of the lesson?

2. In what ways do you think this lesson connects to what students have studied in math before (this school year and before)?

3. How do you think what students learn in this lesson will help them with the math they will learn in the future (this school year and beyond)?

| WORKSHOP 5 | WORKSHEET 5D: TEACHING PRACTICES THAT SUPPORT HIGHER ORDER THINKING |

Think about your focal child (or another child from your classroom). Which of the following teaching practices might work for him or her? How would you use these practices?

Teaching Practices	How would you use these practices with your focal student and other students in your classroom?
Use concept mapping.	
Encourage students to model a problem using diagrams and manipulatives.	
Model problem-solving steps and approaches	
Post a written or pictorial chart that shows the steps for solving problems or for critical thinking.	
Model critical thinking steps and approaches.	
Post a written or pictorial chart that shows the steps for critical thinking.	
Conduct a self-assessment after completion of a problem or activity.	
Have students demonstrate or write about the steps they went through in solving a problem or analyzing an idea.	
Have students work in mixed-ability groups.	
Use problems that are relevant to students' experiences and interests.	
Allow and encourage the use of calculators.	

5.9

Unit Guide for the "Multiplication Cluster Problems" Lesson

UNIT OVERVIEW

Building on Numbers You Know

Content of This Unit Students explore a wide range of strategies for computation and estimation, especially with multiplication and division. They come to recognize that there are many ways to perform each operation: by reasoning about multiples, especially 10's; by skip counting; by approximating the numbers in a problem to nearby familiar numbers, and then adjusting; or by breaking problems into smaller, more manageable parts. The emphasis throughout is on using what they already know about number relationships and the meaning of the operations. Students also use estimation, both before calculating and after, to check the reasonableness of their results. In an Excursion, students get a sense of larger numbers as they "count" to 1 million by 5000's while putting together a display of a million dots.

Connections with Other Units If you are doing the full-year *Investigations* curriculum in the suggested sequence for grade 5, this is the fifth of nine units. Your class will have already had experience with skip counting, multiplication and division, and the composition of large numbers through their work in the unit *Mathematical Thinking at Grade 5*.

If your school is not using the full-year curriculum, this unit can also be used successfully at grade 6.

Investigations Curriculum ■ Suggested Grade 5 Sequence

Mathematical Thinking at Grade 5 (Introduction and Landmarks in the Number System)

Picturing Polygons (2-D Geometry)

Name That Portion (Fractions, Percents, and Decimals)

Between Never and Always (Probability)

▶ *Building on Numbers You Know* (Computation and Estimation Strategies)

Measurement Benchmarks (Estimating and Measuring)

Patterns of Change (Tables and Graphs)

Containers and Cubes (3-D Geometry: Volume)

Data: Kids, Cats, and Ads (Statistics)

Investigation 1 ▪ Exploring Distance Between Numbers

Class Sessions	Activities	Pacing
Session 1 (p. 4) REASONING ABOUT MULTIPLES	Counting by Multiples of 100 Starting at Different Numbers Homework: How Many People Counted? Extension: Counting Backward to 0	minimum 1 hr
Session 2 (p. 12) COUNTING PUZZLES	What's the Counting Number? What's In Between? Homework: What's In Between? Extension: Make Your Own Puzzles Extension: Finding All the Counting Numbers	minimum 1 hr
Sessions 3 and 4 (p. 17) EXPLORING PATTERNS OF MULTIPLES	Sharing Puzzle Solutions Finding Multiples of 21 Making a Tower of Multiples of 21 Using Multiples to Solve Problems Homework: Different Ways to Count Homework: Using Multiples to Solve Problems	minimum 2 hr
Session 5 (p. 27) MULTIPLE TOWERS	Teacher Checkpoint: More Multiple Towers Homework: Multiple Towers	minimum 1 hr
Sessions 6 and 7 (p. 29) THE DIGITS GAME	Introducing the Digits Game Playing the Digits Game Homework: Playing the Digits Game Homework: Problems from the Digits Game	minimum 2 hr
Session 8 (p. 36) SUBTRACTION STRATEGIES	Strategies for Subtraction Teacher Checkpoint: Solving Subtraction Problems Homework: More Digits Game Practice	minimum 1 hr

🕐 **Ten-Minute Math ▪ What Is Likely?**

Mathematical Emphasis	Assessment Resources	Materials
▪ Skip counting by 2-, 3-, and 4-digit numbers between any two 4- or 5-digit numbers ▪ Relating repeated addition (or skip counting) to multiplication ▪ Using skip counting patterns to help solve multiplication and division problems ▪ Developing, explaining, and comparing strategies for subtracting 4- and 5-digit numbers ▪ Recording computation strategies using words, numbers, and arithmetic symbols ▪ Reading, writing, and sequencing 4- and 5-digit numbers	Recording Strategies (Teacher Note, p. 8) What About Notation? (Teacher Note, p. 10) Reasoning About Skip Counting (Dialogue Box, p. 11) Counting the Number of Counting Numbers (Dialogue Box, p. 16) Developing Computation Strategies That Make Sense (Teacher Note, p. 23) 11,000: Even or Odd? (Dialogue Box, p. 25) How Many 21's Are in 945? (Dialogue Box, p. 26) Teacher Checkpoint: More Multiple Towers (p. 27) Observing the Students (p. 31) Helping Students Think About Subtraction (Teacher Note, p. 34) Strategies for Subtraction (Dialogue Box, p. 35) Teacher Checkpoint: Solving Subtraction Problems (p. 37)	Stick-on notes Adding machine tape Tape Envelopes or rubber bands Overhead projector Calculators Student Sheets 1–9 Teaching resource sheets Family letter

Unit Overview ▪ **I-13**

5.11

Investigation 2 ■ Multiplication and Division Situations

Class Sessions	Activities	Pacing
Sessions 1 and 2 (p. 42) MULTIPLICATION AND DIVISION STRATEGIES	The Ringle, an Imaginary Coin Teacher Checkpoint: Boxes of Markers Homework: Zennies Homework: My Coin Extension: Ringles and Dollars Extension: International Currency	minimum 2 hr
Session 3 (p. 50) DIVISION STRATEGIES	Writing Division Equations Strategies for Division Homework: A Division Problem	minimum 1 hr
Session 4 (p. 57) WHAT SHOULD WE DO WITH THE EXTRAS?	Division Situations Homework: Division Situations	minimum 1 hr
Sessions 5 and 6 (p. 61) RELATING MULTIPLICATION TO DIVISION	Homework Review Multiplying with Cartons of Milk Dividing with Cartons of Milk Writing a Multiplication Situation Writing a Related Division Situation Homework: Mimi's Mystery Multiple Tower Homework: Relating Multiplication and Division Situations Extension: Making Sense of Division Situations	minimum 2 hr
Session 7 (Excursion)* (p. 66) PROBLEMS ABOUT OUR SCHOOL	Supplies for Our School Problems About Things in Our School Homework: A Problem About Large Quantities Extension: How Long Would Our Supplies Last? Extension: Package Sizes	minimum 1 hr

⏱ Ten-Minute Math ■ What Is Likely?

* Excursions can be omitted without harming the integrity or continuity of the unit,
but offer good mathematical work if you have time to include them.

Mathematical Emphasis	Assessment Resources	Materials
■ Developing, recording, and comparing strategies for solving multiplication and division problems ■ Making sense of remainders ■ Understanding relationships between multiplication and division ■ Understanding how multiplication and division can represent a variety of situations ■ Modeling situations with multiplication, division, and other operations	Teacher Checkpoint: Boxes of Markers (p. 44) Observing the Students (p. 44) Explaining and Comparing Procedures (Teacher Note, p. 47) Strategies for Division: How Many Ringles? (Dialogue Box, p. 49) Remainders, Fractions, and Decimals (Teacher Note, p. 54) Creating Your Own Multiplication and Division Problems (Teacher Note, p. 55) Helping Students Think About Operations (Teacher Note, p. 56) What Should We Do with the Extras? (Teacher Note, p. 60)	Stick-on notes Metersticks or rulers Packages of school supplies Chart paper Overhead projector (opt.) Bulletin board and tabletop surface Calculators (opt.) Student Sheets 10–19 Teaching resource sheets

I-14 ■ *Building on Numbers You Know*

Investigation 3 ■ Ways to Multiply and Divide

Class Sessions	Activities	Pacing
Sessions 1, 2, and 3 (p. 74) MULTIPLICATION CLUSTERS	Making Close Multiplication Estimates Reasoning About Estimates Multiplication Clusters Multiplication Cluster Strategies Making a Problem Cluster Homework: Writing About Multiplication Clusters Homework: Writing Multiplication and Division Situations	minimum 3 hr
Sessions 4, 5, and 6 (p. 83) DIVISION CLUSTERS	Making Close Division Estimates Reasoning About Division Estimates Teacher Checkpoint: Looking at Division Clusters Solving Division Clusters Making a Division Cluster Homework: Division Cluster Problems Homework: A Division Situation Homework: A Cluster of Problems	minimum 3 hr
Sessions 7, 8, and 9 (p. 91) HOW DID I SOLVE IT?	Practice with Estimating Solving a Problem with the First Step Given How Did I Solve It? Sharing Our Solution Strategies Homework: Two Ways Homework: My Own How Did I Solve It? Problem Homework: Another How Did I Solve It? Problem	minimum 3 hr
Session 10 (p. 100) WAYS TO MULTIPLY AND DIVIDE	Assessment: Ways to Multiply and Divide	minimum 1 hr

◐ Ten-Minute Math ■ Quick Images

Mathematical Emphasis

- Developing, explaining, and comparing strategies for estimating and finding exact answers to multiplication and division problems

- Recording strategies for solving multiplication and division problems

- Solving multiplication and division problems in more than one way

- Using relationships between multiplication and division to help solve problems

Assessment Resources

Observing the Students (p. 78)

Observing the Students (p. 79)

Estimation: Emphasizing Strategies (Teacher Note, p. 81)

About the Cluster Problems in This Unit (Teacher Note, p. 82)

Teacher Checkpoint: Looking at Division Clusters (p. 85)

Observing the Students (p. 86)

Thinking About Remainders (Dialogue Box, p. 90)

Choosing Strategies for Computation (Teacher Note, p. 97)

How Can 6×10 Help Us Solve $133 \div 6$? (Dialogue Box, p. 98)

Assessment: Ways to Multiply and Divide (p. 100)

Assessment: Ways to Multiply and Divide (Teacher Note, p. 102)

Materials

Stick-on notes

Overhead projector

Chart paper

Student Sheets 20–30

Teaching resource sheets

Unit Overview ■ **I-15**

Investigation 4 ■ A Million Dots (Excursion)*		
Class Sessions	**Activities**	**Pacing**
Session 1 (p. 108) ARRAYS OF DOTS	How Many Dots on a Page? Rectangles with 10,000 Dots How Many Dots in All? Homework: Counting Up and Down from 10,000 Extension: Counting to Say Large Numbers Extension: Counting to Say 0 Extension: Factor Pairs of 100,000	minimum 1 hr
Session 2 (p. 115) HOW BIG IS A MILLION?	How Big Is a Million? The Million Dots Display Are We Close to a Million? Homework: Our Million Dots Display Extension: How Long Would It Take to Count to a Million?	minimum 1 hr

* Excursions can be omitted without harming the integrity or continuity of the unit,
  but offer good mathematical work if you have time to include them.

Mathematical Emphasis	**Assessment Resources**	**Materials**
■ Developing a sense of quantities in the thousands, ten thousands, and hundred thousands	Have We Reached a Million Yet? (Teacher Note, p. 119)	Scissors Tape Stick-on notes Calculators
■ Using a rectangular array model to represent factor pairs of numbers 10,000 and larger		Chart paper (opt.) Overhead projector Overhead pens and blank transparencies (opt.)
■ Developing a sense of the size of 1,000,000		Student Sheets 31–33 Teaching resource sheets

5.14

Investigation 5 ▪ Understanding Operations

Class Sessions	Activities	Pacing
Sessions 1 and 2 (p. 122) THE ESTIMATION GAME	Estimating Answers to Difficult Problems Introducing the Estimation Game Playing the Estimation Game Homework: The Estimation Game	minimum 2 hr
Session 3 (p. 128) SOLVING DIFFICULT PROBLEMS	Teacher Checkpoint: How Do We Solve Difficult Problems? Homework: Another Division Problem	minimum 1 hr
Sessions 4, 5, and 6 (p. 130) EXPLORING OPERATIONS	Choice Time: Exploring Operations Discussion: How Did I Solve It? Discussion: How Many Sheets of Paper? Homework: A Multiplication Problem Homework: How Can This Help? Homework: Different Paths to 10,000 Extension: Rewriting Multiplication Expressions Extension: How Many Factors? Extension: Multiplication and Division Practice	minimum 3 hr
Session 7 (p. 139) ASSESSING STUDENTS' UNDERSTANDING	Assessment: Solving Harder Problems How Far to a Million? Choosing Student Work to Save	minimum 1 hr

● Ten-Minute Math ▪ Quick Images

Mathematical Emphasis

- Applying computation strategies to more difficult problems, including both numeric and situational problems

- Developing strategies for estimating answers to difficult multiplication and division problems

- Reading, writing, and sequencing multiples of 5000 up to 1,000,000

- Developing a sense of the size of 1,000,000

- Understanding relationships among the four basic operations

Assessment Resources

Observing the Students (p. 127)

Teacher Checkpoint: How Do We Solve Difficult Problems? (p. 128)

Observing the Students (p. 134)

A Challenging Problem: 37×86 (Dialogue Box, p. 138)

Assessment: Solving Harder Problems (p. 139)

Choosing Student Work to Save (p. 140)

Assessment: Solving Harder Problems (Teacher Note, p. 141)

Materials

Class clock or watches with second hands

Overhead projector

Chart paper

Calculators

Student Sheets 34–41

Teaching resource sheets

Unit Overview ▪ **I-17**

5.15

WORKSHOP 5   LESSON MATERIALS

MATERIALS LIST

Following are the basic materials needed for the activities in this unit.

- Calculators: at least 1 per pair
- Adding machine tape (1 roll)
- Envelopes or rubber bands
- Metersticks or rulers: 1 per pair
- Tape
- Scissors: 1 per pair
- Stick-on notes: 3 packages of 3-by-3-inch or larger notes
- Overhead projector
- Packages of supplies from around the school, in quantity, to use for real-world multiplication and division situations
- Chart paper
- Class clock or watches with second hands
- Bulletin board and tabletop surface

The following materials are provided at the end of this unit as blackline masters. A Student Activity Booklet containing all student sheets and teaching resources needed for individual work is available.

Family Letter (p. 155)

Student Sheets 1–41 (p. 156)

Teaching Resources:
    Numeral Cards, pages 1–3 (p. 165)
    300 Chart (p. 178)
    How Many Dots? (p. 197)
    Million Dots Display Sheet (p. 198)

Practice Pages (p. 213)

Related Children's Literature

Chwast, Seymour, *The 12 Circus Rings*. San Diego: Harcourt Brace, 1993.

McKissak, Patricia C. *A Million Fish . . . More or Less*. New York: Knopf, 1992.

Schwartz, Amy. *Annabelle Swift, Kindergartner*. New York: Orchard, 1988.

Schwartz, David. *If You Made a Million*. New York: Lothrop, Lee and Shepard, 1989.

Note: Some of the blackline masters or student activities for this unit are not included in this book.

ABOUT THE MATHEMATICS IN THIS UNIT

One emphasis of the *Investigations* curriculum is the development of good number sense. This unit continues that emphasis, focusing on computation and estimation skills—especially in multiplication and division, but also in subtraction and addition. As students solve both numeric and situational problems, they develop a wide range of strategies for both estimating and computing.

Through this unit, students come to see that there are many ways to perform each operation. They learn how these different strategies work; they explore relationships among them; they learn to use them flexibly, with a variety of problems; and they consider which strategies are most efficient for particular problems. Some students will develop many strategies; others just a few. The more strategies students come to understand well, the richer their sense of operations will be and the more choices they will have when solving problems.

As they develop their computation strategies, students find ways to use what they already know and understand well, such as familiar factor pairs, multiples of 10, skip-counting patterns, relationships among numbers, and problems they can solve easily. For example, to solve the problem $674 \div 32$, a student might use one of these strategies:

> *Strategy A:* Since $10 \times 32 = 320$, $20 \times 32 = 640$. Add another 32, and you get 672, so $21 \times 32 = 672$ and $672 \div 32 = 21$. Then 674 is 2 more, so $674 \div 32$ is 21 with 2 left over.

> *Strategy B:* You can break the problem into easier division problems. $320 \div 32 = 10$. Double that, and you get $640 \div 32$ equals 20. You're left with $34 \div 32$. You can think of that as $32 \div 32$ equals 1 and $2 \div 32$ equals $\frac{1}{16}$. Put them together and you get $21\frac{1}{16}$.

> *Strategy C:* 32 plus 32 is 64. Since two 32's are 64, twenty 32's are 640. Twenty-one 32's are 672, and 674 is 2 more, so the answer is 21 R 2.

Some of the procedures students try will not be efficient at first, and like any algorithm will require practice before students achieve fluency. Part of your role is to evaluate students' procedures, help

them develop more efficient ones, and support them in practicing those procedures until they become fluent.

Students also develop a variety of ways to determine whether their solutions make sense. For example, students might solve a problem in more than one way and cross-check the answers. They might make up a situation using the numbers in the problem: "We have 674 pencils and want to share them equally among the 32 students in the class. How many will each student get? What will we do with the leftovers?" They might interpret the problem in words before solving it: "How many 32's are in 674?" Or they might make an estimate and see if their answer is in the ballpark.

With estimating, as with finding exact solutions, students develop a variety of strategies. One student might estimate the answer to $674 \div 32$ by rounding both numbers up:

> 32 is close to 35 and 674 is close to 700, and there are 20 35's in 700.

Another might arrive at the same answer by rounding both numbers down:

> 32 is close to 30 and 674 is a little more than 600, and there are 20 30's in 600.

A third might reason this way:

> There are twenty 32's in 640, so the answer to $674 \div 32$ is a little more than 20.

Much of students' initial work with multiplication and division in this unit involves problems with numbers such as 21, 36, 75, and 120—numbers that are familiar from earlier work with factors and multiples. When students work with numbers they understand well and know how to take apart and put together in different ways, they can concentrate on the *meaning* of operations and on finding strategies that make sense to them.

As the unit progresses and students' sense of multiplication and division grows, they apply their strategies to problems involving larger or less familiar numbers, such as 29, 89, 254, 767, and 1904. By the end of the unit, students have ways to solve a wide range of difficult computation problems. In an optional Excursion, students create a display of a million dots and develop a better sense of 6- and 7-digit numbers. This provides a foundation for computation with larger numbers.

The communication of students' thinking and reasoning plays a crucial role throughout this unit. Students learn to keep careful records of the steps they take in solving problems, and they learn to explain their strategies so that others can understand them. As students share their strategies verbally and in writing, they learn to clarify their thinking, to use mathematical notation correctly and unambiguously, to compare strategies and find relationships among them, and to listen to and learn from their peers.

One goal of this unit is that students develop both mental approaches and paper-and-pencil strategies they can rely on for solving problems they will encounter in daily life. A skill they will need is knowing how to break problems into parts, or into convenient subproblems that they can solve mentally or on paper. Therefore, many times in this unit students are asked to solve problems *without* calculators. At other times, in this unit and throughout the school year, students can be encouraged to use calculators as one of many problem-solving tools.

Keep in mind that in order to use calculators appropriately, students need a strong understanding of the four operations and of the number system, so that they can select suitable calculations and determine what a reasonable result might be. As students develop facility with a variety of strategies for computation, they will learn to move fluently between calculators and mental arithmetic and between mental arithmetic and paper-and-pencil methods as they choose approaches for solving problems.

At the beginning of each investigation, the Mathematical Emphasis section tells you what is most important for students to learn about during that investigation. Many of these understandings and processes are difficult and complex. Students gradually learn more and more about each idea over many years of schooling. Individual students will begin and end the unit with different levels of knowledge and skill, but all will gain a deeper understanding of the four basic operations and how to perform them.

ABOUT THE ASSESSMENT IN THIS UNIT

Throughout the *Investigations* curriculum, there are many opportunities for ongoing daily assessment as you observe, listen to, and interact with students at work. In this unit, you will find five Teacher Checkpoints:

Investigation 1, Session 5:
More Multiple Towers (p. 27)

Investigation 1, Session 8:
Solving Subtraction Problems (p. 37)

Investigation 2, Sessions 1–2:
Boxes of Markers (p. 44)

Investigation 3, Sessions 4–6:
Looking at Division Clusters (p. 85)

Investigation 5, Session 3:
How Do We Solve Difficult Problems? (p. 128)

This unit also has two embedded Assessment activities:

Investigation 3, Session 10:
Ways to Multiply and Divide (p. 100)

Investigation 5, Session 7:
Solving Harder Problems (p. 139)

In addition, you can use almost any activity in this unit to assess your students' needs and strengths. Listed below are questions to help you focus your observation in each investigation. You may want to keep track of your observations for each student to help you plan your curriculum and monitor students' growth. Suggestions for documenting student growth can be found in the section About Assessment.

Investigation 1: Exploring Distance Between Numbers

■ Are students able to skip count by 2-, 3-, and 4-digit numbers? How comfortable are they with skip counting between any two 4- and 5-digit numbers? How do they make predictions about counting sequences?

■ Do students relate skip counting and multiplication? Do they see multiplication as repeated addition?

■ Do students use skip-counting patterns to solve multiplication and division problems?

■ How do students solve subtraction problems with 4- and 5-digit numbers? Do they choose a

particular strategy depending on the problem? How do they record and explain their strategies? Do they compare their strategies with those of other students? Do they ever adopt another's strategy?

■ How do students record their strategies for solving computation problems? Do they use words? numbers? arithmetic symbols? some combination of these? Are they solving and recording problems in more than one way? Do they find some strategies to be easier than others?

■ How comfortable are students with reading, writing, and sequencing 4- and 5-digit numbers?

Investigation 2: Multiplication and Division Situations

■ What strategies are students developing for solving multiplication and division problems? Do they choose a particular strategy based on the problem? How do they record and compare their work? Do they ever adopt another's method?

■ How do students make sense of and deal with remainders? Do they describe the remainder in the context of the problem?

■ What relationships are students finding and using between multiplication and division? How comfortable are they using multiplication to solve a division situation or a problem presented in division notation?

■ Do students understand that multiplication and division notation can represent a variety of situations? Are they able to give examples of problems for which you would use multiplication, and others where division would be used?

■ How do students model situations with multiplication? division? other operations?

Investigation 3: Ways to Multiply and Divide

■ How do students make estimates to multiplication and division problems? On what do they base their estimates? Do they use landmarks or familiar numbers? Are their estimates reasonable? What strategies do they use to find exact answers to those problems? Can students refine their estimation strategy to solve a problem exactly? Are students able to explain their strategies? Are they comparing these strategies with other students'?

■ How are students recording their strategies for solving multiplication and division problems? Can you follow students' strategies by looking at their work?

■ Are students comfortable solving multiplication and division problems in more than one way? Are they keeping track of the steps used to solve the problems? How are they making sense of and recording remainders?

■ Do students recognize relationships between multiplication and division? Do they use those relationships to solve problems?

Investigation 4: A Million Dots

■ Are students developing a sense of the relative size of 1000, 10,000, and 100,000?

■ How comfortable are students with a rectangular array model for representing factor pairs of numbers 10,000 and larger? What strategies did they use to make the rectangles?

■ Are students beginning to develop a sense of the relative size of larger powers of 10? What strategies are they using to estimate how many rectangular arrays or sheets it will take to reach one million dots?

Investigation 5: Understanding Operations

■ How do students solve more difficult numeric problems? Situational problems? Do they apply strategies they've developed over the course of the unit?

■ What strategies are students developing for estimating answers to difficult multiplication and division problems? What information or familiar numbers do they use? Are their estimates reasonable?

■ How comfortable are students reading, writing, and sequencing multiples of 5,000 up to 1,000,000?

■ Are students developing a sense of the size of 1,000,000? What strategies are they using to estimate how many more dots it will take to reach one million?

■ How flexibly do students use the four operations? How comfortably do they move among and relate the four operations?

Assessment Sourcebook

In the *Assessment Sourcebook* you will find End-of-Unit Assessment Tasks and Assessment Masters available in English and Spanish. You will also find suggestions to help you observe and evaluate student work and checklists of mathematical emphases with space for you to record individual student information.

I-22 ■ *Building on Numbers You Know*

Sessions 1, 2, and 3

Multiplication Clusters

Materials

- Student Sheet 20 (1 per student)
- Student Sheet 21 (1 per student, homework)
- Student Sheet 22 (2 per student, homework)
- Students' Multiple Towers (from Investigation 1)
- Stick-on notes
- Chart paper (optional)
- Overhead projector (optional)

What Happens

Students reason about estimating the answers to multiplication problems, considering which strategies give the closest estimates. Then they solve multiplication clusters that offer practice splitting multiplication problems into components that are easier to solve, with particular emphasis on the use of multiples of 10 and 100—that is, seeing 24×31 as $(24 \times 10) + (24 \times 10) + (24 \times 10) + 24$. Students also write and solve their own multiplication cluster problems. Student work focuses on:

- using familiar multiplication problems to estimate answers to unfamiliar multiplication problems
- using familiar multiplication problems (especially those involving multiples of 10) to solve unfamiliar multiplication problems
- splitting multiplication problems involving 2- and 3-digit numbers into more manageable components

Ten-Minute Math: Quick Images The Quick Images activity provides valuable practice in spatial concepts. Two or three times during this investigation, outside of math time, use the overhead to present a geometric design. Use three or four Power Polygons, pattern blocks, or other regular polygons, leaving small spaces between the polygons so that students can identify the individual shapes. For example:

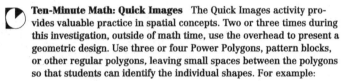

Flash the pattern for 3 seconds and then cover it while students try to recreate the design themselves. They might use their own set of shapes, or draw what they saw. Flash the design for another 3 seconds and let students revise their work. When most students have finished, show the design again and leave it visible for further revision. If students are having difficulty, suggest that they try to find the familiar shapes that make up the figure.

After students finish a design, encourage them to talk about what they saw in successive flashes. You may hear comments such as "I saw a long box with wings." During this discussion, introduce correct terminology for the shapes (*parallelograms, octagons, trapezoids,* and so forth). As you use the terms naturally, students will begin to recognize and use the terms themselves.

For variations on the Quick Images activity, see p. 149.

Activity

Making Close Multiplication Estimates

Write the problem 27 × 8 on the board.

When we solve a problem like this one, we can make a close estimate as a way of beginning. How would you estimate the answer to this problem? Would the answer be more than 100? more than 200? more than 300? What helps you make an estimate?

As students share their strategies for estimating, record them on the board. Strategies may fall into these categories:

- Using familiar multiplication pairs:

  Half of 8 is 4 and there are 4 25's in 100. If you double that you get 200. So, it's about 200.

  The answer is a little less than 240 because 27 is a little less than 30, and 30 × 8 is 240.

  It's between 200 and 240 because you can round 27 off to 25 or 30. If it's 25 then it multiplies out to 200, and if it's 30, it's 240.

- Using multiples of 10:

  I know 27 × 10 is 270, so the answer is a little less than 270.

  It's about 200 because 10 × 8 is 80, and double it is 160, and then you have to add on the 7 × 8.

- Breaking the problem into more familiar components:

  I know 12 × 8, so I said it's close to 12 × 8 + 12 × 8 because 12 and 12 is 24. That's 196.

Students with limited estimating experience may think that estimating is the same as "rounding off." That is, they may try to find the exact answer first, then approximate it to a round number. The **Teacher Note,** Estimation: Emphasizing Strategies (p. 81), suggests ways to help students approach estimation more meaningfully.

After they have discussed their estimates, students find the exact answer to 27 × 8 (without standard algorithms or calculators), then share solution strategies.

Repeat the activity with 27 × 13. If students are having difficulty making estimates, offer them familiar round numbers to think about, as you did in the previous problem:

Is it more than 100? more than 500?

You might also ask if the answer to the previous problem could help them estimate the answer to 27 × 13.

Sessions 1, 2, and 3: Multiplication Clusters ■ **75**

5.22

Activity

Reasoning About Estimates

I'm going to give you a multiplication problem and two possible ways to estimate the answer. Talk with a partner about which way would give a closer estimate. See if you can decide *without doing any calculations,* even in your head.

Write the following on the board or chart paper:

    Problem: 47 × 32   Estimates: 40 × 32 50 × 32

As students talk in pairs, circulate to remind them to decide which estimate is closer *without* doing any calculations; that is, without finding the answers to 40 × 32 or 50 × 32. Ask a few volunteers to share their thinking with the class. For example:

    50 × 32 is a closer estimate because it is three 32's away from the answer, and 40 × 32 is seven 32's away.

    50 is closer to 47 than 40 is, so 50 × 32 is a closer estimate.

    I would round to 50 if the number was more than 45, and 40 if it was less than 45.

If you think your students need more practice, repeat the activity with another problem and two estimates that involve changing only one of the numbers in the problem. For example:

    Problem: 22 × 17   Estimates: 20 × 17 25 × 17

More Challenging Problems Next present a problem and two estimates, each of which involves changing a *different* number in the problem. For example:

    Problem: 39 × 22   Estimates: 40 × 22 39 × 20

Again, students determine which estimate is closer to the exact answer without doing any calculations. Encourage them to think about how many more or less than the exact answer the estimates are.

Is 40 × 22 larger or smaller than 39 × 22? How many more 22's larger? Is 39 × 20 larger or smaller? How many more 39's smaller?

Continue to repeat the activity, asking questions as needed to encourage the same kind of thinking.

    Problem: 312 × 9   Estimates: 312 × 10 300 × 9
    Problem: 123 × 38   Estimates: 123 × 40 120 × 38

Activity

Multiplication Clusters

Before starting this activity, have the Multiple Towers from Investigation 1 posted where students can see them. Some of the problems in this activity (and throughout the rest of this investigation) involve numbers for which students built towers. Students may always refer to the Multiple Towers if it helps them to solve those problems.

Introducing Cluster Problems Write the following cluster of problems on the board. Students with previous experience in the unit *Mathematical Thinking at Grade 5* or in the *Investigations* grade 4 curriculum will be familiar with cluster problems. See the **Teacher Note**, About the Cluster Problems in This Unit (p. 82), for background information.

$$10 \times 32 \qquad 5 \times 32$$
$$20 \times 32 \qquad 30 \times 32$$
$$35 \times 32$$

This is a cluster of multiplication problems. In a cluster, you can use relationships among the problems to help you find the answers. For example, the first four problems here can help you find an answer to the last one (35×32). Try it. If you think another problem will help you solve 35×32, add it to the cluster.

Working with a partner, students first make an estimate for 35×32, then solve all the problems. They may refer to the Multiple Towers, but they may not use standard algorithms or calculators.

Circulate as students work. Encourage them to think about which multiplication pairs they "just know," and when they need to apply a strategy to find the answer. After students have been working for several minutes, call the class together to talk about relationships among the problems in the cluster.

How can knowing $10 \times 32 = 320$ help you to solve 5×32? How can knowing 10×32 help you to solve 20×32? Which of the problems in this cluster helped you to figure out the answer to 35×32? Are there other problems not in this cluster that might have helped you?

Add 36×32 to the cluster. Ask students to explain how the answer to 35×32 can help them with 36×32.

Working on Multiplication Clusters Give each student a copy of Student Sheet 20, Multiplication Cluster Problems. Students may work alone or in pairs. Remind them to use relationships among the problems to solve the *last* problem in the cluster. Students may refer to the Multiple Towers, but may not use standard algorithms or calculators.

Sessions 1, 2, and 3: Multiplication Clusters ▪ **77**

5.24

Observing the Students   While students are working, observe what strategies they have for relating known factor pairs to new multiplication problems. Remind students to add to the cluster any other problems that help them solve the last problem in the cluster.

- Do they use multiplication by multiples of 10 to solve problems? For example, do they solve 47 × 18 by thinking (10 × 18) + (10 × 18) + (10 × 18) + (10 × 18) + (7 × 18)? Can they relate 2 × 72 to 20 × 72?

- Do they use doubling and halving to find solutions? For example, to solve 5 × 18, do they use 10 × 18 = 180, then halve 180? Or do they think of 20 × 18 as double 10 × 18?

- Can they put together answers to two or more easier problems to solve a more difficult one? (40 × 18 is 720, and 5 × 18 is 90, so 45 × 18 is 810). Do they see how to use subtraction as well as addition to solve multiplication problems, for example, thinking of 498 × 9 as (500 × 9) – (2 × 9)?

- Do they have strategies for determining whether an answer makes sense? Do they use estimation? Do they try solving the problem in a different way? Do they make up a multiplication situation to fit the problem?

- What factor pairs do they know by heart?

If some students are having difficulty solving cluster problems, you might want to work with them in a small group. Encourage these students to talk about how they can use what they know to solve more difficult problems. Students may find it helpful to make an estimate of the answer to the final problem in the cluster, or another problem in the cluster they find difficult. As students make an estimate using multiplication pairs they are familiar with, they may begin to see ways that they can use what they know to solve more difficult problems.

If you feel that some students are ready for harder problems, or conversely that the problems on Student Sheet 20 are too difficult for some students, adjust the numbers.

Students who finish early can find a different way to solve the final problem in each cluster, or they can build a Multiple Tower for a number no one has explored yet (perhaps 29, 68, 77, 85, 154, 281, 326, 543, or 1233).

Activity

Multiplication Cluster Strategies

Write the second cluster from Student Sheet 20 on the board.

10 × 18	5 × 18
50 × 18	2 × 18
20 × 18	40 × 18
45 × 18	47 × 18

Ask students to describe ways they used the problems in the cluster to find the answer to 47 × 18. What other problems *not* in this cluster might have helped them?

Following are some possible strategies for solving 47 × 18:

■ Breaking the problem into 40 × 18 and 7 × 18, and adding the two results. Students might solve 7 × 18 by breaking it into 5 × 18 and 2 × 18, or by counting up by 18's from 5 × 18.

■ Finding the result of 50 × 18 and counting down by 18's.

■ Recognizing that 45 × 18 is 9 times 5 × 18. Students multiply the result of 5 × 18 by 9, and then add on 2 × 18.

As students explain their strategies, draw their attention to examples that involve multiplying by 10, doubling, and partitioning larger numbers into smaller or more familiar components. Many students will see a pattern when a number is multiplied by 10. They may notice that you always add a zero and be unable to explain why. Encourage students to doublecheck their work using other strategies. They should be able to estimate that their answer is a reasonable one. For example, if a student solves 20 × 18 by saying that "It's like 2 × 18, but it's 20, not 2, so you add 0 and get 360," you might ask "And how do you know 360 is a reasonable answer? Is there another way you can prove it? How do you know it's not 3600?"

Activity

Allow at least 30 minutes at the end of Session 3 for this activity. Write on the board or overhead:

26 × 31

Making a Problem Cluster

Students work with a partner to create their own cluster of several problems that would help them find the answer to 26 × 31 without using algorithms or calculators. They solve all the problems in their cluster.

If students are having difficulty getting started, ask two or three volunteers to suggest a problem that might help them think about how to solve 26 × 31. Record these ideas as the students briefly explain how each problem might help. The clusters that student pairs write may include some or all of the problems on the board.

Observing the Students   As students work, circulate to observe what strategies they are using. Are they beginning with familiar factor pairs? reasoning about multiples of 26 or 31? skip counting? using relationships among factor pairs? partitioning numbers into two or more components? Encourage any students having difficulty to use strategies that involve multiplying one of the factors by 10.

Sessions 1, 2, and 3: Multiplication Clusters ■ **79**

5.26

As pairs finish, they write their clusters on the board or post them on a bulletin board. Set aside about 5 minutes for students to look at each other's sets, to see if they can understand why the authors chose these particular problems. They might post stick-on notes with their initials on any sets they do not understand; resolve any such questions in a brief whole-group discussion.

The student who wrote the above cluster explained it this way: "To figure out 26 × 31 you can add up the answers to 20 × 31 and 5 × 31 and 1 × 31 because 20 + 5 + 1 = 26. I started with 10 × 31 because I knew it automatically. Then 20 × 31 is double 10 × 31, so add 310 + 310. And 5 × 31 is half of 10 × 31, so divide 310 by 2. You get 25 × 31 by adding the answers to 20 × 31 and 5 × 31. Then add 1 more 31 to get 26 31's."

Sessions 1, 2, and 3 Follow-Up

Homework

Writing About Multiplication Clusters After Session 1, students complete Student Sheet 21, Writing About Multiplication Clusters. Collect these papers so you can get a sense of how students are thinking about cluster problems.

Writing Multiplication and Division Situations After Session 2, students write a multiplication situation based on the final problem in one of the clusters they have solved. They record the problem they choose on Student Sheet 22, Writing Multiplication and Division Situations. Then they write a division situation that corresponds to their multiplication situation and write the equation with division notation. After Session 3, send home another copy of Student Sheet 22 for more practice.

❖ **Tip for the Linguistically Diverse Classroom** Students can use pictures with symbols and words to communicate their multiplication and division situations.

Students might ask an adult to solve their multiplication situation *without* using a standard algorithm or calculator. Students can then demonstrate how they used the problems in the cluster to find the answer.

Estimation: Emphasizing Strategies   ◁ Teacher Note

Estimating is an important skill with useful applications both in and out of school. Practicing and talking about estimation develops good number sense and can also help students develop strategies for performing exact calculations. When students estimate, they use relationships among numbers that are familiar to them. For example, to estimate the answer to 27×8, students might think of $25 \times 8 = 200$, $27 \times 10 = 270$, or $30 \times 8 = 240$. Any of these familiar relationships can serve as fruitful starting places for exact calculations.

Some students believe that an estimate must be a "round" number, or that a better estimate is one that is closer to the answer. When asked to estimate the answer to 27×8, some students will first find the exact answer, 216, and then approximate it to a number such as 200, 210, or 220. These students are not estimating; they are simply approximating numbers.

Here are some ways that you can help students approach estimation in a meaningful way and recognize the importance of estimation:

■ As students discuss their strategies, draw their attention to approaches that yield estimates expressed as *less than* or *more than* rather than exact numbers. For example: "The answer to 27×8 is a little less than 240 because 27 is a little less than 30, and 30×8 is 240."

■ When students are sharing estimation strategies, focus the discussion on how they made their estimates rather than how close their estimates are to the exact answer. That way, students will not be tempted to first find the exact answer and then share an "estimation" strategy that yields a closer answer. To help students evaluate different estimation strategies, present a problem and two or three strategies for estimating the answer. Ask students if they can determine which would yield a closer estimate and why, without doing any calculations. For example: "Which is a closer

estimate for the answer to 47×32: 40×32 or 50×32? Why?" Encourage reasoning such as "50×32 is a closer estimate because it is three 32's away from the answer, while 40×32 is seven 32's away."

■ Ask students to estimate as part of the problem-solving process. Making an estimate *first* can help them determine the reasonableness of the answer they find by exact calculation (with or without a calculator). Similarly, making an estimate *after* solving a problem can give them a sense of whether their answer is about right.

■ Help students recognize that how close an estimate needs to be depends on why they are estimating. For example, if you notice a student has an extra 0 at the end of an answer (having written 8700 instead of 870), ask for an estimate of the answer. Explain that in this case, it doesn't matter whether the estimate is off by 1, 10, or even 25; it is valuable simply because it shows that the calculated answer is too large.

■ Encourage students to think of situations where an estimate is sufficient (perhaps because an exact answer is unnecessary, difficult, or impossible to find) and to think about how close an estimate should be in each such situation. For example, if we are about to go to the grocery store and want to know if we have enough money to buy everything on our shopping list, we might make an estimate of the total cost. If we are planning a party, we might make estimates based on the number of guests: how much we think they will eat, and how much that amount of food will cost. Many people in business, like carpenters, house painters, and landscapers, need to make estimates when bidding a job to determine what materials they will need and how much they will cost.

Sessions 1, 2, and 3: Multiplication Clusters ■ **81**

Name _____

Date _____

Student Sheet 20

Multiplication Cluster Problems

Solve each cluster of problems. Look for ways that
the problems in each cluster are related.

10 × 123	20 × 123
2 × 123	**22 × 123**

10 × 18	5 × 18
50 × 18	2 × 18
20 × 18	40 × 18
45 × 18	**47 × 18**

400 × 9	500 × 9
90 × 9	8 × 9
2 × 9	**498 × 9**

2 × 72	10 × 72
5 × 72	20 × 72
200 × 72	**210 × 72**
215 × 72	

179

Investigation 3 • Sessions 1–3
Building on Numbers You Know

5.29

Name _____   Date _____

Writing About Multiplication Clusters

Solve this cluster of problems and write about how you
solved it. Tell how you used one answer to help you find
another answer.

10×21 2×21

5×21 50×21

52×21

180   *Investigation 3 • Sessions 1–3*
Building on Numbers You Know

Name _____   Date _____

Writing Multiplication and Division Situations

Choose the final problem from one of the clusters you
solved and record it here.

_____ × _____

Write a multiplication situation based on the final problem
in the cluster.

Now write a division situation that relates to the multiplication situation you wrote above. Write the equation using
division notation.

Investigation 3 • Sessions 1–3
Building on Numbers You Know

181

Plan and implement a math lesson that supports students' higher order thinking functions.

- Select a lesson that you will teach over the next month. Consult with the colleagues in your team. Read the description of the lesson and enact it with your colleagues (actually do the work of the lesson; don't just think about how it will be done). Analyze the goals and the higher order thinking demands of the lesson. Take notes in the second column of the Lesson Planning Chart.
- Think about the strengths and needs of one or more focal children, and take some notes about how you expect the child or the children to respond to the higher order thinking demands of the task. Add your notes in the third column of the Lesson Planning Chart (if you need more space, use extra copies of the chart).
- Together with the colleagues in your team, plan some adaptations for the lesson that address the higher order thinking strengths and needs of the students. Record your ideas in the fourth column of the Lesson Planning Chart.
- Implement the lesson with the adaptations. If possible, invite the members of your team to observe the lesson. (You may want to videotape the focal child so that you and your colleagues can examine him or her as a team.) Have one or more members of your team observe your focal child(ren). Record your observations on the Observation Chart.
- Answer the lesson analysis questions.

WORKSHOP 5	WORKSHEET 5E: LEARNING GOALS

Your Name: _____ Focal Student Pseudonym:_____

Name of the Lesson: _____

Review the introductory pages for the lesson (and its unit) you are planning to help you answer the questions below.

1. What are the learning goals of the lesson?

2. In what ways do you think this lesson connects to what students have studied in math before (this school year and before)?

3. How do you think what students learn in this lesson will help them with the math they will learn in the future (this school year and beyond)?

5.33

WORKSHOP 5   **WORKSHEET 5F: HANDS-ON EXPLORATION OF THE MATH ACTIVITY**

Read the description of the lesson and enact it with your colleagues. It is important to actually carry out the focal activity of the lesson. Don't just think about how it will be done.

Observe and reflect on what **higher order thinking** you need to use to carry out this activity. Please use the space below to jot down your observations/reflections.

Your Name: _____   Focal Student Pseudonym: _____

Name of Activity or Lesson Explored: _____

Learning Areas (based on Barringer et al., 2010; Levine, 2002; Pohlman, 2008)	What are the demands of the lesson activity? What roles do these learning areas play in the lesson activity?	How will the focal child(ren) respond to the demands of the activity? Please note strengths and needs below.	How could you change the lesson to make it more accessible to all students, including the focal student(s)?
Higher Order Thinking			
• **Thinking with concepts** (a concept may be abstract, concrete, a process, verbal, or nonverbal)			
• **Problem solving** (involves knowing it's a problem, previewing outcomes, assessing feasibility, mobilizing resources, logical thinking, strategies, starting and pacing, self-monitoring, dealing with impasses, and reflecting)			
• **Critical thinking** (involves knowing the facts, the creator's point of view, your point of view, errors, and exaggerations and getting outside help, weighing the evidence, and communicating)			
• **Rule-guided thinking** (if...then kinds of thinking)			
• **Creative thinking** (involves divergent thinking, taking a fresh look, suspension of self-evaluation, and risk taking)			

Language • understanding mathematical language • using language to communicate with others and to clarify one's ideas						
Spatial Ordering • interpreting relationships within and between spatial patterns • organizing things in space • reasoning with images						
Sequential Ordering • organizing information in sequence • following directions • managing time						
Memory • short-term memory • active working memory • long-term memory						
Attention • controlling mental energy • maintaining focus • self-monitoring						
Psychosocial • using and understanding social language • collaboration • conflict resolution						
Motor Coordination • gross motor functions • fine motor functions • grapho-motor functions						

Higher Order Thinking

Your Name: _____　　Focal Student Pseudonym: _____

Name of Activity or Lesson Explored: _____

Learning Areas (based on Barringer et al., 2010; Levine, 2002; Pohlman, 2008)	How did the focal student handle the various demands of the activity or lesson? Note your observations below.
Higher Order Thinking	
• **Thinking with concepts** (a concept may be abstract, concrete, a process, verbal or nonverbal)	
• **Problem solving** (involves knowing it's a problem, previewing outcomes, assessing feasibility, mobilizing resources, logical thinking, strategies, starting and pacing, self-monitoring, dealing with impasses, and reflecting)	
• **Critical thinking** (involves knowing the facts, the creator's point of view, your point of view, errors, and exaggerations and getting outside help, weighing the evidence, and communicating)	
• **Rule-guided thinking** (if...then kinds of thinking)	
• **Creative thinking** (involves divergent thinking, taking a fresh look, suspension of self-evaluation, and risk taking)	
Language • understanding mathematical language • using language to communicate with others and to clarify one's ideas	

5.37

Spatial Ordering
- interpreting relationships within and between spatial patterns
- organizing things in space
- reasoning with images

Sequential Ordering
- organizing information in sequence
- following directions
- managing time

Memory
- short-term memory
- active working memory
- long-term memory

Attention
- controlling mental energy
- maintaining focus
- self-monitoring

Psychosocial
- using and understanding social language
- collaboration
- conflict resolution

Motor Coordination
- gross motor functions
- fine motor functions
- grapho-motor functions

Your Name: _____ Focal Student Pseudonym: _____

1. What changes did you and your team make to the original lesson?

2. What do you think students learned? Did they reach the goal(s) of the lesson?

3. Did the students do what you expected them to do? Were there any surprises? Were there any students who didn't participate fully?

4. Did your focal student work as you had hoped he or she would?

5. In what ways did the changes you and your team made to the lesson help the focal student? Did these changes help other students as well?

6. If you were to teach or assist with this lesson again, what would you do differently?

7. How has this assignment influenced your work with students (or teachers)?

Appendix A

Learning Goals

Your Name: _____ Focal Student Pseudonym: _____

Name of the Lesson: _____

Review the introductory pages for the lesson (and its unit) you are planning to help you answer the questions below.

1. What are the learning goals of the lesson?

2. In what ways do you think this lesson connects to what students have studied in math before (this school year and before)?

3. How do you think what students learn in this lesson will help them with the math they will learn in the future (this school year and beyond)?

Appendix B

Accessible Lesson Planning Chart

Your Name: _____ Focal Student Pseudonym: _____

Name of Activity or Lesson Explored: _____

Learning Areas (based on Barringer et al., 2010; Levine, 2002; Pohlman, 2008)	What are the demands of the lesson or activity? What roles do these learning areas play in the lesson or activity?	How will the focal child(ren) respond to the demands of the task? Please note strengths and needs below.	How could you change the lesson to make it more accessible to all students, including the focal student(s)?
Higher Order Thinking • using and forming concepts • solving problems • logical thinking • creative and critical thinking			
Language • understanding mathematical language • using language to communicate with others and to clarify ideas			

(Continued)

(Continued)

Learning Areas (derived from Barringer, M. D., Pohlman, C., & Robinson, M. 2010. *Schools for all kinds of minds.* San Francisco, CA: Jossey-Bass)	What are the demands of the lesson or activity? What roles do these learning areas play in the lesson or activity?	How will the focal child(ren) respond to the demands of the task? Please note strengths and needs below.	How could you change the lesson to make it more accessible to all students, including the focal student(s)?
Spatial Ordering • interpreting relationships within and between spatial patterns • organizing things in space • reasoning with images			
Sequential Ordering • organizing information in sequence • following directions • managing time			
Memory • short-term memory • active working memory • long-term memory			
Attention • controlling mental energy • maintaining focus • self-monitoring			
Psychosocial • using and understanding social language • collaboration • conflict resolution			
Motor Coordination • gross motor functions • fine motor functions • grapho-motor functions			

Appendix C

Lesson Analysis Questions

1. What changes did you/your team make to the original lesson?

2. What do you think students learned? Did they reach the goal(s) of the lesson?

3. Did the students do what you expected them to do? Were there any surprises? Were there any students who didn't participate fully?

4. Did your focal student work as you had hoped he or she would?

5. In what ways did the changes you/your team made to the lesson help the focal student? Did these changes help other students as well?

6. If you were to teach or assist with this lesson again, what would you do differently?

7. How has this assignment influenced your work with students?

CORWIN

A SAGE Company

The Corwin logo—a raven striding across an open book—represents the union of courage and learning. Corwin is committed to improving education for all learners by publishing books and other professional development resources for those serving the field of PreK–12 education. By providing practical, hands-on materials, Corwin continues to carry out the promise of its motto: **"Helping Educators Do Their Work Better."**

The mission of Bank Street College is to improve the education of children and their teachers by applying to the educational process all available knowledge about learning and growth, and by connecting teaching and learning meaningfully to the outside world. In so doing, we seek to strengthen not only individuals, but the community as well, including family, school, and the larger society in which adults and children, in all their diversity, interact and learn. We see in education the opportunity to build a better society.

Education Development Center, Inc.

EDC tackles some of the world's most urgent challenges in education, health, and economic development. For half a century, we have collaborated with public and private partners to design, deliver, and evaluate program innovations in the United States and around the world. Using a powerful combination of research, strategy, and training, EDC advances formal and informal education, health promotion and care, workforce preparation, communication technology, and civic engagement.